Uncovering Your Mind

How the Brain Learns and Adapts

Dr. Henry Oh

Foreword by Dr. Gabriel Lopes
President, Logos University International
France, Brazil, USA

Published by Amazon Publication Experts
San Jose
California

First Edition, September 2024
ISBN:
Library of Congress Control Number:
Cover design by Courtney Roberts

Printed in the United States of America

Disclaimer: The information provided in this book is for educational purposes only. The author and publisher are not responsible for any adverse effects or consequences resulting from the use of any of the suggestions, preparations, or procedures discussed in this book. All matters pertaining to your health should be supervised by a health care professional.

Table of Contents

Foreword vii

Preface ix

Acknowledgements xi

Dedication xii

About the Author xiv

A Welcome Message xvi

Self-Assessment Questionnaire xviii

Prologue xxi

CHAPTER 1 1

The Nervous System and The Brain 1

- Fascinating Facts About the Brain 1
- The Nervous System 2
- Human Brain: The Body's Control Center 6
- Synaptic Plasticity and Synaptogenesis in Learning and Memory 12
- Other Interactions of Synaptic Plasticity and Synaptogenesis in Cognitive Processes 14
- Brain Regions 14
- Physiological and Biochemical Processes 16
- in the Brain 16

CHAPTER 2 19

The Process of Learning 19

- Factors Influencing Learning 20

Boosting Motivation 22
Examples of Different Learning Experiences 23
Maslow's Hierarchy of Needs and Learning 24
Linking Maslow's Hierarchy to Learning 26
Integrating Maslow's Hierarchy in Education 28
The Learning Pyramid 29
How the Brain Changes 31
CHAPTER 3 33
Sleep, Brain Waves, Circadian Rhythm, and Relaxation . 33
The Importance of Sleep for Learning and Memory 33
What Happens During Sleep? 33
How Sleep Makes Learning Easier 34
Brain Waves in Learning, Memory, and Storage 37
Circadian Rhythm for Learning 40
Relaxation Strategies 43
CHAPTER 4 46
Attention, Learning, Memory and Consolidation 46
Factors Affecting Attention Span 46
Learning Strategies 47
Enhancing Memory and Retention 49
Consolidation of Learning Across Lessons 52
CHAPTER 5 57
Cramming, Test Anxiety, Note-Taking & Reviewing...... 57
The Dangers of Cramming: Cognitive Overload.......... 57
Strategies to Prevent Cramming 59

Dealing with Test Anxiety 60
Psycho-Behavioral Strategies and Their Benefits......... 64
Effective Notetaking 67
Reviewing After Class 69
CHAPTER 6 75
Neuroplasticity:.. 75
The Brain's Ability to Adapt 75
An Overview of Neuroplasticity 75
Brain Rewiring.. 77
Leveraging Neuroplasticity for Learning...................... 79
Breaking Free from Limiting Beliefs............................ 84
Case Study on Overcoming Addiction and Mental Barriers.. 86
CHAPTER 7 87
Neuroplasticity in Selected Cases 87
Neuroplasticity and ADHD: The Connection............... 87
Helping Students with ADHD 89
Case Study on ADHD 92
Neuroplasticity and Brain Injury 94
Real-Life Examples of Recovery 96
Case Study on Head Injury 97
Post-Traumatic Stress Disorder (PTSD)....................... 99
Cognitive Behavioral Therapy (CBT) 101
Eye Movement Desensitization and Reprocessing (EMDR) 102
Case Study on PTSD.. 103

Dementia and Alzheimer's Disease 105
Neuroplasticity and Aging 108
CHAPTER 8 111
Future Frontiers of Learning 111
Advances in Neuroscience and Learning 111
Research in Dementia and Alzheimer's Disease 112
Implications for Education and Training 113
EPILOGUE 116
Finding My Way Back: My Success Story 116
The Brain's Power to Learn, Adapt, and Heal 117
Student Engagement, Retention and Success 118
Hidden Disabilities 119
APPENDIX A 120
Scoring and Interpretation 120
Recommendations Based on Results 122
APPENDIX B 123
Brain Learning and Adaptation Q&A 123
APPENDIX C 131
A Research Study 131
REFERENCES 135

Foreword

Welcome to a journey into the remarkable world of neuroscience with "Uncovering Your Mind: How the Brain Learns and Adapts." I have devoted many years to studying the complexities of the human brain and am thrilled to introduce this intellectually stimulating exploration of how we learn and adapt.

In our fast-paced world, understanding how our brains function and adapt is critical. This book provides essential insights into the mechanics of learning, memory, and neuroplasticity, making it a valuable resource for students, teachers, and anyone dedicated to lifelong learning.

I have known the author, Dr. Henry Oh, for several years, and I can say with certainty that Henry's expertise and enthusiasm for the subject permeate this book. It combines research with practical implications, allowing readers of all levels of understanding to grasp complex ideas.

Henry is not only an esteemed figure in the field of health sciences but also has a rich background in teaching, leadership, innovation, and research. His ability to translate intricate scientific knowledge into readable and engaging content is unrivaled.

Sua abordagem inovadora e compromisso com a excelência é admirável, refletido não apenas em sua própria carreira brilhante, mas também em sua capacidade de motivar e inspirar os colegas ao seu redor. Dr. Henry Oh é um profissional por excelência. (Portuguese-Brazil)

(His innovative approach and commitment to excellence is admirable, reflected not only in his own brilliant career but also in his ability to motivate and inspire the colleagues around him. Dr. Henry Oh is a professional par excellence.)

I hope you read on with an open mind and a sense of curiosity. In addition to deepening your appreciation of the brain, I hope this book helps you see the extraordinary potential for learning and growth that your brain possesses. Enjoy and learn!

Prof. Gabriel César Dias Lopes, PsyD, PhD, EdD
President
Logos University International
France, Brazil, USA

Preface

In this book, I aim to explain how incredible the brain is, how it works, adapts, and changes, and how it is involved in intricate processes like learning, memory, and cognitive development.

Whether you are a student studying the brain, an academic, or someone simply interested in the brain, I will guide you through the fascinating and sometimes challenging steps involved in acquiring knowledge and skills. For those in neuroscience or dedicated to studying the brain, this book offers a fresh perspective that can enhance their understanding and inspire further research.

Chapter 1 begins with a discussion of the structure of the brain and its functions. This includes an overview of neurons, synapses, and neurotransmitters, all of which are crucial for communication within the brain. You will find a list of amazing facts about the brain in this chapter.

In the subsequent chapters, you will learn about the learning process and the stages of memory, including acquisition, encoding, storage, and retrieval, which are essential for acquiring, storing, and remembering information.

One of the most appealing aspects of this book is the information about neuroplasticity, or how the brain can change over time. It shows how neuroplasticity can benefit learning and how the brain can recover following an injury. It is imperative to know how the brain can change based on what we do, practice, and experience, including recovery from injury.

Furthermore, we will explore aspects of learning that have a physical and bodily component, including the role of sleep, exercise, and nutrition in maintaining a healthy brain. There are recommendations on how to deal with test anxiety, cognitive overload or cramming.

The final chapters of the book shift focus more to the future and explore some fascinating developments in neuroscience and what they might mean for education and training. Real-life examples and stories are employed to create a personal learning experience that makes brain science more understandable and relevant.

There is a self-assessment questionnaire designed to help you assess your learning styles, emotional regulation, attention span, and overall cognitive health. The scoring, interpretation and recommendations are found on Appendix A. Appendix B contains 15 questions on the topic, while Appendix C includes the first three pages of a published research study conducted by our team on synaptic plasticity and collaborative learning for enhanced cognition.

My overall goal is for you to have a new appreciation for how amazing your brain is and to provide strategies on how you can maximize its potential.

Thank you.

Dr. Henry Oh

Acknowledgements

This work could not have been completed without the support of many individuals. I wish to thank my colleagues at Logos University and Laramie County Community College for providing a supportive academic environment, and especially to my family, whose encouragement, love and support were central to writing this book.

A special thank you goes to my former students, Cooper Mickelson, who shared his testimony about his academic journey in the prologue of this book, and to Chance Torres, who also shared his story in the epilogue of this book.

Thank you also to my mentors, past and present, for sharing their ideas and knowledge. What I learned from them has been reflected in this book.

Finally, I would like to thank Dr. Gabriel Lopes, Dr. Eugene Demekhin, Dr. LaVerne Adekunle, and Dr. Howard Vince Oh, with whom I have worked on several projects, research studies, and special occasions. They have motivated me to write this book. There are not enough words to describe my gratitude for their expertise, input, support, patience, and precious time.

Dr. Henry Oh

Dedication

To my late parents, Henry Oh, Sr., and Vicenta Saavedra Oh, whose love and support have been the foundation of my journey. Your unwavering belief in me continues to inspire and guide my path.

To my family, for your endless patience, encouragement, and understanding. Your presence is my strength and motivation.

To my adopted mother, Mary Torres, whose kindness and care have been a beacon of strength in my life.

To my fellow Ateneans, Thomasians, and Josepheans, your camaraderie, support, and shared experiences have been instrumental in my journey.

To my mentors, whose wisdom and guidance have shaped my understanding and passion for the sciences of the brain, cardiopulmonary and clinical laboratory. Your teachings have been invaluable.

To my fellow educators, for your dedication to the pursuit of knowledge and your commitment to shaping the minds of future generations.

To my students, for your curiosity and enthusiasm. You are the reason this book has been written, and you continue to be my greatest teachers.

To future generations of students, leaders, and educators, may you continue to explore, innovate, and inspire. Your potential knows no bounds.

In gratitude,
Henry

"Success is nothing without sharing it with the ones you love- family and friends."

Aloha Ke Akua

Bishop Ernest Silva, Jr., SSD

About the Author

Dr. Henry Oh is an established educator, leader, and scholar in the field of health sciences. He has served as a speaker at state, national, and international seminars and conferences in the U.S., as well as overseas, in South America and Southeast Asia. He has held academic leadership positions in several colleges and universities.

As an educator, Dr. Oh is focused on student success, utilizing a holistic approach when preparing students for their national certification exams. His method includes cognitive preparation, study techniques, mental health and physical conditioning. He keeps his students engaged in a supportive classroom environment where coursework is both challenging and aligned with exam standards. He addresses individual learning styles and fosters a network of support, enabling students to stay motivated and focused on their academic goals.

Dr. Oh holds several certifications, including Certified Brain Fitness Coach (CBFC), Board-Certified Mental Health Coach (BCMHC), Registered Respiratory Therapist with Neonatal Pediatric Specialty (RRT-NPS), and Certified Medical Laboratory Scientist (MLS). He also holds certifications in the U.K. and Europe as a Chartered Biologist (CBiol), Chartered Scientist (CSci), and European

Professional Biologist (EurProBiol) from the European Countries Biologists Association (ECBA).

He has previously served as the president of the Lambda Beta Honor Society for Respiratory Care, president of the New Mexico AMT State Society, vice president of the Utah AMT State Society, and Chairman (Governor-appointed) of the New Mexico Respiratory Care Licensing Board.

Dr. Oh has been recognized with numerous national and international awards, including the International Distinguished Scholar in 2024, U.S. Professor of the Year in Health Sciences in 2020, Asia Pacific Excellence Award for Outstanding Achiever in Medicine and Allied Sciences in 2017, Editor of the Year in 2014 from the American Medical Technologists (AMT), and Master Teacher of Honor from Kappa Delta Pi (KDP) International Honor Society in Education in 2013.

He is a self-taught pianist who generously shares his musical talent at fundraising events, cultural gatherings, dinner receptions, senior homes, and dementia care facilities.

A Welcome Message to Students, Teachers, and Anyone Dedicated to Lifelong Learning

Welcome to a fascinating world—the world of brain, learning, and rewiring!

In our journey, we will scrutinize the incredible complexity of everything that happens in our brains as they receive, organize, and retrieve information. Just as importantly, we will examine the basic underpinnings of our brains—neurons, synapses, and neurotransmitters.

Understanding these basic components can help us understand why we learn and remember as we do. The information will be presented with practical examples and general accessibility to make the material both informative and resonant. We will then leave all this information on the page and provide practical strategies for learning.

Whether you are a reader who wants to learn more about how you learn and grow, a student trying to break bad habits, or a teacher who wants to better understand why your students learn as they do, I hope you can find some illumination in the process of understanding your brain.

I wrote this book in an outline format for easier reading, learning, and finding information later.

But wait!

Before we dive into the fascinating world of brain function, learning, and neuroplasticity, let's start with a quick self-assessment.

The questionnaire is designed to help you understand your unique learning preferences, emotional regulation strategies, attention span, and cognitive health habits. By identifying these aspects early on, you can tailor the strategies and insights from this book to your personal needs, making your learning journey more effective and enjoyable.

Let's get started!

Henry

Self-Assessment Questionnaire

Below is a 12-item questionnaire designed to help you assess your learning styles, emotional regulation, attention span, and overall cognitive health.

Section 1: Learning Styles

1. When learning new information, which method do you find most effective?
   a) Reading text and viewing diagrams
   b) Listening to lectures or audio recordings
   c) Hands-on activities and practice

2. How do you prefer to organize your study material?
   a) Written notes and highlighted texts
   b) Recording and listening to summaries
   c) Creating models or using physical objects

3. What type of environment helps you concentrate the best?
   a) Quiet and isolated
   b) Background music or ambient noise
   c) Active and dynamic settings

Section 2: Emotional Regulation

4. How often do you feel anxious before a test or exam?
   a) Almost always
   b) Sometimes
   c) Rarely

5. Which strategies do you use to manage stress?
   a) Deep breathing or meditation
   b) Talking to someone or seeking support
   c) Physical exercise or hobbies

6. How do you handle setbacks or poor grades?
   a) I feel discouraged and struggle to move forward
   b) I reflect on what went wrong and try to improve
   c) I quickly move on and focus on the next task

Section 3: Attention and Focus

7. How long can you concentrate on a task before needing a break?
   a) Less than 20 minutes
   b) 20-40 minutes
   c) More than 40 minutes

8. What techniques do you use to maintain focus during study sessions?
   a) Scheduled breaks (e.g., Pomodoro Technique)
   b) Changing subjects or tasks periodically
   c) Using incentives or rewards

9. How often do you find yourself distracted during lectures or study sessions?
   a) Frequently
   b) Occasionally
   c) Rarely

Section 4: Cognitive Health

10. How many hours of sleep do you get on average per night?
    a) Less than 6 hours
    b) 6-8 hours
    c) More than 8 hours

11. How often do you engage in physical exercise?
    a) Rarely
    b) 1-3 times a week
    c) More than 3 times a week

12. How balanced is your diet in terms of brain-boosting foods (e.g., fruits, vegetables, nuts)?
    a) Poorly balanced
    b) Moderately balanced
    c) Well-balanced

End of Questionnaire

For scoring, interpretations, and recommendations, please see Appendix A on page 125.

Prologue

This testimonial, provided by a former student, details his academic journey. He made notable improvements in his studies, successfully completed the program, and passed the national certification examination. He has granted permission to include this letter in this book.

Dear Dr. Oh,

I want to give my heartfelt thanks to you for your incredible support and mentorship during my time at the university. When I think back to my time spent in the program for Respiratory Therapy, I can see how much you helped shape my journey and personal development. When I first came to the university, excited to be there and ambitious to take advantage of all the educational opportunities, that changed quite quickly. I wasn't able to focus and didn't put the effort into listening during class and studying. It was more than a little bit of an inconvenience, in fact, it was a big deal.

My inability to focus was going to be the barrier to the future I saw for myself academically. Not only did I struggle with the material, I felt overwhelmed by the assignments and I always seemed to be behind in everything we were doing. The period was full of frustration and doubt in myself. The doubts were about my abilities and my presence in the world of academia.

You took the time to understand what was happening with me. You let me talk about what wasn't working, without a word of judgement, and missing were any feelings of inadequacy. You offered real suggestions and personalized tips to help me focus more and also manage my time smartly.

What I remember about you working with me is that you recommended I reach out to other students and resources like tutoring and counseling.

Your approach to holistic education, that you cared about me as a person/student, was warm and so needed. The advice you gave me about focusing and paying attention, and having a plan to manage my time was both really helpful. After following your strategies, I began to see a significant improvement. My grades were consistently improving, and I found myself more interested and motivated in my coursework.

I still remember, Dr. Oh, your commitment to your students and passion for teaching. The lasting impression you made on my life is a gracious gratitude expressed for your unmatched support and influence on my academic journey. I was able to not only pass the national exam and received my RRT, but I also completed my bachelor's with a high GPA.

Thank you for believing in me, for your patience, and for your unwavering commitment to helping me succeed.

Respectfully,
Cooper Mickelsen, BSRT, RRT

CHAPTER 1

The Nervous System and The Brain

Fascinating Facts About the Brain

1. The covering that keeps our brain safe is called the cranium or skull, which is made of 22 bones.

2. Although the brain weighs about 2% of a person's body weight, it needs 20% of the body's energy and oxygen intake.

3. The human brain is 30 times faster than the IBM Sequoia, one of the fastest supercomputers in the world.

4. If the brain does not get oxygen for 5 minutes, some brain cells die, causing brain damage.

5. The number of brain cells is close to 100 billion, referred to as neurons.

6. 20% of the blood that leaves the heart is sent to the brain to fuel the neurons.

7. The brain is made up of 73% water; less than 2% water loss may cause deficient attention, memory, and cognitive skills.

8. The brain has more than 100,000 biochemical reactions per second.

9. The energy produced in the brain is generated from glucose from the body.

10. The brain produces enough electrical energy to light a small electric bulb.

11. The brain creates new connections with every new learning.

12. To remember something and have a good memory, you need proper sleep every night. During sleep, the brain stores the memories from the day.

13. Stress may change the brain's shape and how the brain functions.

14. Our brains hold 25% of the cholesterol in our body. Our brains have the most fat in the body; approximately 60% of the brain is made from fat.

15. Consuming alcohol may stop the brain from making new memories.

(Alban & Alban, 2024)

The Nervous System

Before investigating the intricacies of the brain, it is important to examine the larger environment in which it functions: the nervous system. The nervous system is the principal conduit of communication in the body, managing the essential function of transmitting information between parts of the body and coordinating actions. By understanding the nervous system, we can better understand the specific functions and abilities of the brain, which we will discuss later.

The nervous system is a complex network responsible for controlling the body, consisting of two main components:

The Central Nervous System (CNS) and The Peripheral Nervous System (PNS).

A. Central Nervous System (CNS)

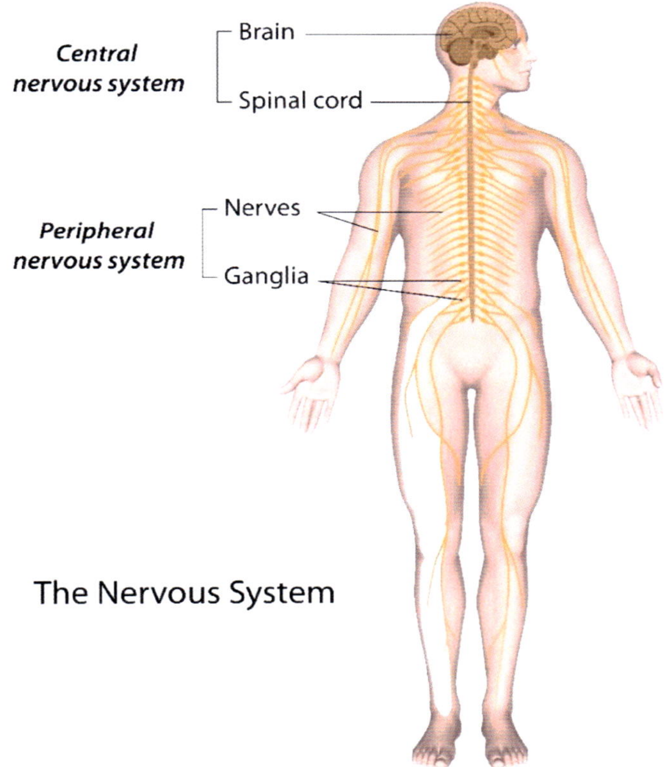

The CNS comprises the brain and spinal cord.

- **Brain**:
  The brain serves as the control center of the body, handling senses, movement, thoughts, emotions, and memories.

- **Spinal Cord:**
  The spinal cord is a long, thin, tubular structure made up of spinal nerves. It

connects the brain to the rest of the body and monitors and controls simple reflex responses without involving the brain.

- **Function**:
  The CNS examines sensory information from the body, decides how the body should react, and then sends the appropriate instructions. It also organizes information received from multiple sources within and outside the body and manages any actions that need to be performed.

B. Peripheral Nervous System (PNS)
The PNS consists of all nerves that extend from the CNS and connect it to the body. The PNS is divided into two major subdivisions:

- **Somatic Nervous System (SNS):**
  The SNS controls voluntary movements and sends sensory information back to the CNS. It is responsible for activities that are physically or voluntarily controlled, such as walking or any activity requiring muscle movement.

- **Autonomic Nervous System (ANS):**
  The ANS controls involuntary activities in the body, such as heart contraction, digestion and respiration. The ANS is further subdivided into the Sympathetic Nervous System and the Parasympathetic Nervous System.

  a) The Sympathetic Nervous System:
  This system prepares the body for threats ('fight or flight') by

speeding up the heart rate, increasing blood flow to the muscles, and releasing adrenaline.

b) **The Parasympathetic Nervous System:**
This system supports "rest and digest" functions, slowing the heart rate, increasing intestinal and gland activity, and relaxing sphincter muscles.

C. Key Concepts

- **Neurons**: The basic units of the nervous system that communicate by receiving electrical and chemical signals to transmit information.

- **Neurotransmitters**: Chemicals that carry signals across the synapse from one neuron to the next. Examples include dopamine, serotonin, and acetylcholine.

- **Synaptic Cleft**: The gap between neurons where neurotransmitters are released to transfer information from one neuron to the next.

- **Functions and Integration:**
  Sensory Input: Information gathered from the environment is sent to the brain and spinal cord for processing.

a) **Motor Output:**
Processed information is sent to the muscles and glands via the peripheral nervous system to enact a response.

b) **Homeostasis**:
The autonomic nervous system helps the body maintain homeostasis by controlling involuntary functions such as heart rate, digestion, and respiration.

Human Brain: The Body's Control Center

At the center of the nervous system is the human brain, a unique organ responsible for almost everything our body does. Residing within the cranium, the brain is both fragile and strong, providing us with extraordinary learning abilities and adaptability.

The brain is composed of neurons, which collectively form the nervous system. At a synapse, where one neuron ends and another begins, there is a tiny gap. A neurotransmitter is released across this gap, allowing the electrical impulse traveling along the neuron to reach an adjacent neuron. This signal moves from the end of one neuron through the synapse and into the next neuron.

Neurotransmitters play a crucial role in transmitting signals around the brain, assisting muscle movement, and influencing mood. By understanding neurons, synapses, and neurotransmitters, we gain insights into how the learning can facilitate changes in our brain.

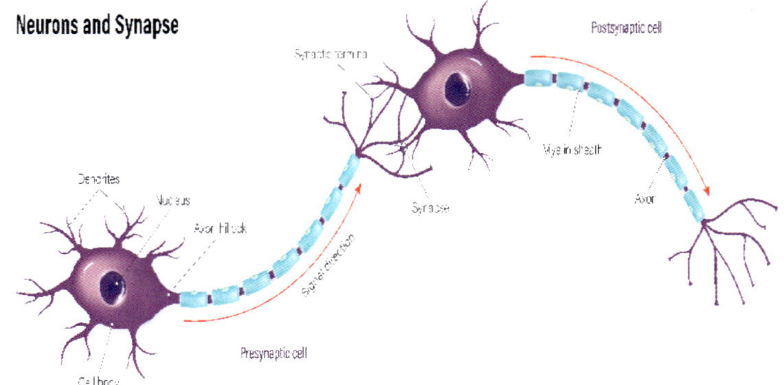

The brain is organized into various sections, each with specific functions. The cerebral cortex, the brain's outer layer, hosts high-level functions associated with voluntary movement, perception, and thought. The hippocampus is essential for memory formation, while the amygdala holds emotional memories. The prefrontal cortex is responsible for executive functions and decision-making.

The brain is the ultimate controller, managing body movements and more. It works continuously, even during sleep, storing memories and preparing for the next day. One of the brain's most fascinating features is its plasticity—the ability to change and adapt to experiences. This adaptability allows for learning, recovery from setbacks, and personal growth.

Understanding the brain's process of learning and adaptation deepens our appreciation for this incredible organ and informs our approaches to learning practices. Exploring the science behind brain function reveals techniques that can improve memory and focus and optimize the brain's capabilities.

Neurons

Neurons are the essential building blocks of the brain that process and communicate information. Neurons are like the brain's mail carriers, small cells conversing with each other to get first-rate work done. Working together, neurons enable you to think, feel, and move. The brain has countless neurons, each with a specific role: some send messages, some receive them, and others help everything function smoothly. When you learn something new or experience emotions like happiness or fear, it's because the neurons in your brain are communicating with each other.

Each neuron has three primary components:

- **Cell Body (Soma)**: Houses the nucleus and other organelles, including attachment points for axons and dendrites, maintaining cellular health.

- **Dendrites**: Extensions from the cell body with branch-like structures that receive messages from other neurons.

- **Axon:** Extends from the cell body and carries messages away from the neurons to other neurons, muscles, or glands.

Neurotransmitters

Neurotransmitters are like special helpers, acting as messengers passing messages between neurons. When neurons communicate, they use special molecules called neurotransmitters. The neurotransmitters are released from the sending neuron and float into the space between the two neurons, called a synapse. When neurotransmitters reach the receiving neuron, the message is passed along. It's like sending a text message to a friend or giving someone a note in class. Neurotransmitters are devoted to transmitting signals across synapses from one neuron to the next. The key neurotransmitters responsible for learning, memory, concentration, and storing information are:

A. **Glutamate**: The primary excitatory neurotransmitter in the brain, essential for synaptic plasticity and long-term potentiation (LTP), which are crucial for strengthening connections between neurons for learning and memory formation. It facilitates the activation of N-methyl-D-aspartate (NMDA) and α amino-3-hydroxy-5-methyl-4-isoxazolepropionic acid (AMPA) receptors, which are key to synaptic transmission and plasticity.

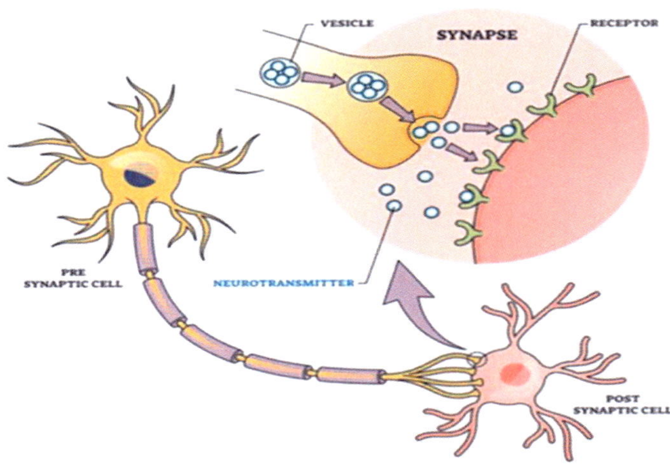

B. **Dopamine**: Closely associated with reward and motivation, dopamine is essential for reinforcement learning. It signals reward, helping to shape new behaviors and habits, and regulates attention and working memory, necessary for maintaining attention and executive functions. Dopamine impacts mood, arousal, and overall cognitive functioning.

C. **Acetylcholine**: Involved in attention and memory, acetylcholine increases synaptic plasticity, particularly in the hippocampus, for encoding new memories. It moderates attention and arousal, which is important for effective learning and concentration.

D. **Serotonin**: Associated with mood regulation, serotonin influences mood, anxiety, and cognition and modulates memory and learning by affecting synaptic plasticity and neurogenesis in the hippocampus. Proper serotonin levels are necessary for maintaining a positive mood and optimal cognitive function.

E. **Norepinephrine (Noradrenaline)**: Involved with alertness and stress response, norepinephrine modulates alertness, arousal, and attention, which is necessary for effective learning and memory consolidation. It also influences emotional memory encoding by affecting activities in the hippocampus and amygdala.

F. **GABA (Gamma-Aminobutyric Acid):** The main inhibitive neurotransmitter in the brain, GABA regulates neural excitability, preventing excessive excitation to ensure cognitive function and focus. Appropriate GABA levels reduce anxiety and promote a calm state conducive to learning.

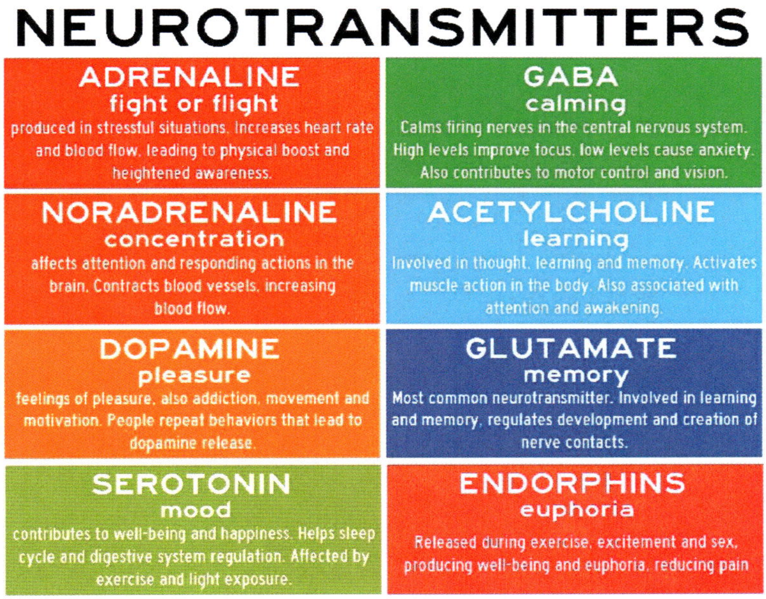

NEUROTRANSMITTERS

ADRENALINE **fight or flight** produced in stressful situations. Increases heart rate and blood flow, leading to physical boost and heightened awareness.	**GABA** **calming** Calms firing nerves in the central nervous system. High levels improve focus, low levels cause anxiety. Also contributes to motor control and vision.
NORADRENALINE **concentration** affects attention and responding actions in the brain. Contracts blood vessels, increasing blood flow.	**ACETYLCHOLINE** **learning** Involved in thought, learning and memory. Activates muscle action in the body. Also associated with attention and awakening.
DOPAMINE **pleasure** feelings of pleasure, also addiction, movement and motivation. People repeat behaviors that lead to dopamine release.	**GLUTAMATE** **memory** Most common neurotransmitter. Involved in learning and memory, regulates development and creation of nerve contacts.
SEROTONIN **mood** contributes to well-being and happiness. Helps sleep cycle and digestive system regulation. Affected by exercise and light exposure.	**ENDORPHINS** **euphoria** Released during exercise, excitement and sex, producing well-being and euphoria, reducing pain

These neurotransmitters work together to modulate various cognitive processes, supporting effective learning, memory consolidation, focus, and information retention. Understanding their role can help develop strategies to enhance cognitive performance and overcome learning challenges.

Synapses

Synapses are like bridges that connect neurons, small spaces where neurons meet or communicate. In your brain, synapses are busy areas where all the actions happen, where messages are passed from one neuron to the next. Think of synapses as busy intersections in a bustling city, with neurons driving to and from, passing information. Synapses play a crucial role in ensuring the brain works correctly. Every time you learn something new, experience emotions, or remember something, it’s because synapses are hard at work helping your brain operate properly.

Synapses are the connections between neurons where communication occurs. When an electrical signal reaches the end of an axon, neurotransmitters are released into the synaptic cleft (the intercellular space between neurons). These neurotransmitters attach to receptors on the neighboring neuron, signaling the next neuron in the process. Learning strengthens these synapses through a coordination of neural connections, referred to as synaptic plasticity. As one learns new ideas, the neural connections become stronger and more efficient, improving thinking and skills.

Synaptic Plasticity and Synaptogenesis in Learning and Memory

Synaptic Plasticity

Synaptic plasticity is defined as the way in which the connections of neurons, or synapses, are strengthened or weakened for a period of time after they have increased or decreased their activity. This level of adaptability is crucial for learning and memory.

A. **Long-term potentiation (LTP):** LTP is a long-lasting increase in synaptic strength that follows high-frequency stimulation of a synapse.

   - **Role in learning and memory**: As a result of LTP, signal transmission between neurons becomes easier, allowing for increased ease in neuron communication. This process is thought to be a cellular mechanism for learning and memory. Learning something new induces long-term potentiation (LTP), reinforcing the neural pathways established during the learning process and enhancing the efficiency of future signal transmissions.

B. **Long-term depression (LTD)**: LTD is a long-lasting decrease in synaptic strength following low-frequency stimulation of a synapse.

- **Role in learning and memory:** LTD weakens less-used synapses, which is important for the removal of old memories and adaptability to learning new information. This synaptic pruning refines neural circuits, enhancing cognitive efficiency and storage capacity.

Synaptogenesis

Synaptogenesis is the formation of new synapses between neurons in the brain. This process mainly occurs during early development but continues throughout life, especially with learning and experiences.

A. **Synaptogenesis in Learning Situation:** Synaptogenesis involves the growth of new connections between synapses stemming from learning new skills or information.

- **Role in learning and memory:** The brain forms new synapses during learning, providing a large capacity for storing new information. This process is critical for creating the neural architecture that supports learning and memory consolidation.

B. **Experience-dependent synaptogenesis:** This type of synaptogenesis advances the development of new synapses due to specific environmental stimuli and experiences.

- **Role in learning and memory:** Experience-dependent synaptogenesis helps the brain incorporate new experiences into learning and memory. For example, learning a new language or mastering a new musical instrument creates new synapses that encode these new skills.

Other Interactions of Synaptic Plasticity and Synaptogenesis in Cognitive Processes

Synaptic plasticity, including LTP and LTD, and experience-dependent synaptogenesis are common in learning curves and memory formation and retrieval. Together, synaptic plasticity and synaptogenesis improve the neural network, enhancing cognitive processes, such as problem-solving, critical thinking, and decision-making.

Conservation of memory in the brain: Synaptic plasticity helps memory formation, and synaptogenesis supports the creation of more synapses throughout life. Understanding these processes helps explain a lifetime of learning and memory. By understanding synaptic plasticity and experience-dependent synaptogenesis, we appreciate the brain's learning and memory processes throughout life.

Brain Regions

The brain consists of different parts, each responsible for specific functions. For instance, the frontal lobe houses the decision-making and planning centers of your brain, and the temporal lobe is primarily responsible for functions like hearing and memory.

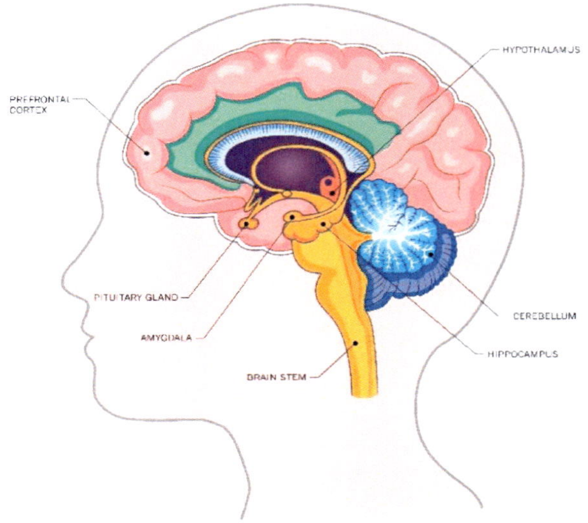

For learning and memory, several brain regions are crucial:

- **Hippocampus**: Essential for forming memories and linking them with emotions and senses. It plays a key role in converting short-term memories into long-term ones.

- **Prefrontal Cortex**: Involved in advanced cognitive behavior, decision-making, and moderating social behavior. It is also necessary for working memory and executive function.

- **Amygdala**: Critical for processing emotions like fear and pleasure and plays a role in memory formation, particularly emotional memories, by enhancing the storage of information.

- **Cerebellum**: Essential for motor learning and coordination and plays a role in cognitive functions such as attention and language.

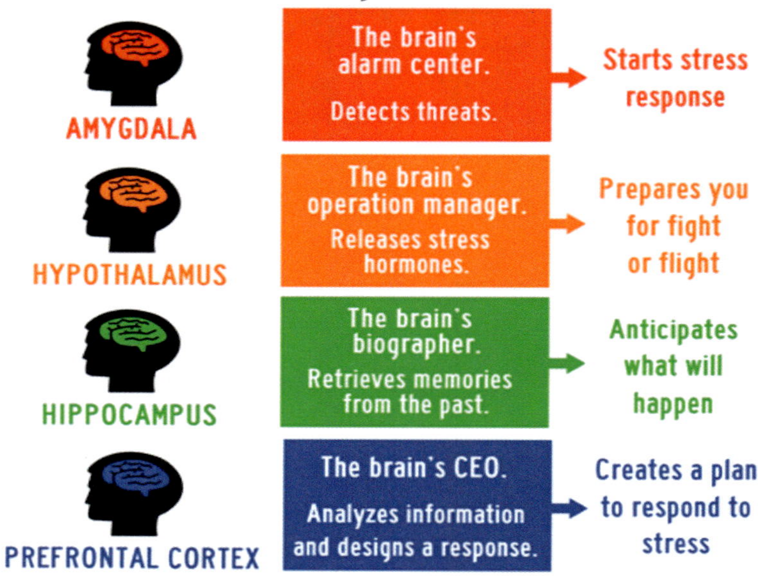

These regions work together as an interconnected network to support various types of learning and memory. Understanding their roles and functions can help develop strategies to enhance learning and improve memory.

Physiological and Biochemical Processes in the Brain

Learning is a complex process involving many physiological and biochemical processes in the brain, allowing individuals to acquire, store, and retrieve information. Key components include:

A. Neurogenesis:
The production of new neurons in the brain, most active during development but continuing in certain areas like the hippocampus throughout adulthood.

B. Hippocampus:
Crucial for long-term memory formation, neurogenesis in the hippocampus enhances learning and memory by integrating new neurons into existing neural circuits.

C. Signal transduction Pathways:
Biochemical reactions resulting in cellular changes, initiated by neurotransmitter binding to receptors, necessary for synaptic plasticity and memory formation.

> **CREB (cAMP Response Element-Binding Protein):** A cellular transcription factor crucial for gene expression regulation, especially during learning, mediating the transcription of genes necessary for synaptic plasticity.
>
> **BDNF (Brain-Derived Neurotrophic Factor):** A protein supporting neuron growth, development, and survival. It is involved in synaptic plasticity and crucial for memory and learning.

D. Structural Changes: Learning is associated with changes in brain structure, such as increasing dendritic spines or reorganization of synapses.

> **Dendritic Spine Formation:** Creating new spines increases the number of synapses, enhancing the brain's capacity for information storage.

Synaptic Pruning: The removal of weaker synaptic connections refines neural circuits, increasing signaling efficiency.

E. **Metabolic Processes**:
Energy metabolism in the brain is critical for learning.

- **Glucose Metabolism**: The brain primarily uses glucose for energy, with greater neuronal activity during learning, increasing glucose consumption.

- **Mitochondrial Function:** Mitochondria produce energy for cells, necessary for processes like signal transduction and synaptic plasticity.

Understanding these physiological and biochemical processes provides insight into how the brain supports learning and memory, helping to develop strategies for enhancing cognitive performance and overcoming learning challenges.

CHAPTER 2

The Process of Learning

Understanding how your brain processes, collects, and stores new information allows you to plan ways to enhance this process. For example, actively engaging with the content, structuring content in meaningful ways, and using retrieval methods like regular review can help you remember what you learned and improve your learning.

Learning is a cycle that occurs in different stages: acquisition, encoding, storage, and retrieval. Each stage plays a crucial role in how we consume, interpret, and remember new information.

A. Acquisition
This is when you encounter new knowledge and determine its relevance. You can think of this stage as picking up parts for a puzzle. When you view a slideshow, read a chapter in a book, or watch a YouTube tutorial, your brain is coming into contact with new data. For example, when learning a recipe, you start by reviewing the ingredients and directions. Your brain processes everything it can at this point, a process called bottom-up processing.

B. Encoding
After watching a video, reading a book, or observing a demonstration, your brain needs to process the information and make it meaningful. Encoding can be compared to translating the information into a code or language that you understand and will remember. Encoding might involve visualizing the steps to cook the recipe or relating them to techniques you already know. It's about organizing and

making sense of the information to facilitate easier retrieval later.

C. Storage

Encoded information requires a place to be stored. Your brain creates physical connections in the form of neural pathways to store and organize this information. Think of this as saving a file on your computer or placing your notes in a folder on your desk. For the recipe, storage happens over time as you practice making it, strengthening the memory trace and making it easier to recall in the future. Through practice, these pathways become more robust, and the information becomes more durable and accessible.

D. Retrieval

Lastly, and importantly, you need to be able to access the stored information when needed. Retrieval is akin to opening a file on your computer or flipping through organized notes to find what you're looking for. For a recipe, retrieval occurs when you can make it without referring to the recipe card. Retrieving information (such as making the recipe) reinforces the memory trace and makes it easier to recall in the future.

Factors Influencing Learning

Learning doesn't just mean reading or doing – there is much more to it. Let's look at key factors that can affect how well you learn: biological, environmental, and emotional influences, as well as some cognitive strategies that can help improve learning.

Biological, Environmental, and Emotional Influences

A. Biological Influences

Genetics: Some people might have a natural inclination towards certain abilities due to their genetic makeup. For example, you might have a musical talent because it is a family trait.

Nutrition: What you eat affects your brain. A healthy diet with lots of fruits, vegetables, and omega-3s may increase brain function. Processed foods and junk food can slow you down and make it harder to focus.

Sleep: Getting enough sleep is important for memory consolidation. Last-minute cramming may seem like a good idea, but in reality, it can significantly interfere with your ability to learn. Aim for 7 to 9 hours of quality sleep to keep your brain in prime condition.

Exercise: Physical fitness isn't just about physical health – it's beneficial for your brain too. Regular exercise can improve memory, focus, and mood, making learning easier.

B. Environmental Influences

Learning Environment: A clean, quiet, well-lit study area can help you focus. Consider setting up a study area that is dedicated to studying without distractions.

Resources: Good resources, such as books, the internet, and knowledgeable people, can assist with your learning process. Don't hesitate to ask for help from a professional or use online platforms to access extra materials.

Technology: Technology can be a distraction or a helpful learning tool. Educational apps, online courses, and interactive simulations are a few of the ways you can learn and understand information in a different way.

C. Emotional Influences

Stress: Stress can be a distraction and can also reduce your ability to focus and remember information. To help manage stress, practice mindfulness or meditation and take regular breaks when studying.

Student Motivation: Being personally interested in what you are learning is unquestionably important. You can facilitate greater motivation by linking class material to your own interests or goals.

Support Systems: Surround yourself with positive friends, family, and mentors who can encourage you to continue gaining knowledge. Your support system can also share knowledge and insights.

Boosting Motivation

A. Finding Your "Why"

Understand the reason behind your studies or work. Ask the question, "Why am I doing this?" Determine what your goals are, whether they are personal, academic, or professional.

B. Reward Yourself

Reward yourself for completing tasks or reaching milestones. These rewards can be as small as a treat, or as large as taking a break to watch TV or go out with friends.

C. Stay Optimistic

Maintain a positive outlook to boost your motivation. Surround yourself with supportive people, practice positive self-talk, and focus on your successes rather than your mistakes.

D. Make a Schedule

A steady routine helps create a habit of studying, making it easier to stay motivated. Use a planner or digital calendar to schedule study time and follow through.

E. Change Up How You Study
Changing up your study strategies can keep studying interesting. Be creative: make flashcards, involve friends in a study group, master the content well enough to explain it to someone else, or use a variety of multimedia resources.

F. Stay Physically Active
Engage in physical activity often, as regular exercise can boost your mood and energy levels, increasing motivation. Even a short walk can make a difference.

Examples of Different Learning Experiences

The following examples illustrate how new information is acquired, encoded, stored, and retrieved in various learning experiences:

Learning a New Language
Sarah, a college student, decides to learn Spanish before her study abroad trip to Spain. She attends Spanish classes and uses language learning apps to practice. While exploring the streets of Barcelona, one of her dream destinations, she decides to eat at a local restaurant and orders entirely in Spanish. Despite initial nervousness, she successfully communicates with the waiter. This real-world application not only improves her language skills but also boosts her confidence in using Spanish in practical situations.

Mastering a Musical Instrument
Alex, a high school student, is determined to learn how to play the guitar. He spends countless hours practicing chords and melodies, often feeling discouraged by challenging solos. However, after weeks of persistent effort, he finally masters the solo of his favorite song. The sense of accomplishment reinforces his belief that hard work and dedication pay off, giving him a deeper understanding of

perseverance and the rewarding feeling of mastering a skill through practice.

Learning through Hands-On Experience
Emily, a student passionate about cooking, is working toward a pastry certificate in a culinary arts program. Instead of just studying from textbooks, she spends most of her time experimenting with dough and recipes in the kitchen. One day, she accidentally adds too much sugar to a pastry dough, making it overly sweet and sticky. Rather than getting discouraged, she improvises and revises the recipe. Through this hands-on experience, Emily learns the value of problem-solving, creativity, and practical learning.

Real-Life Problem-Solving
James, a recent graduate, lands his first job in IT support. On his first day, he encounters a complex technical issue he's never seen before. Initially feeling defeated, he recalls a similar problem from his certification course. He calmly works through the problem step-by-step, using his knowledge and critical thinking skills. His successful resolution impresses his peers and reinforces the importance of applying theoretical knowledge to real-world scenarios and maintaining a calm demeanor under pressure.

These examples highlight the diverse ways people learn—whether it's acquiring a new language, developing a musical skill, engaging in hands-on learning, or solving real-life problems. Despite different paths, the common themes of persistence, determination, and enjoyment of the journey lead to personal growth and skill development.

Maslow's Hierarchy of Needs and Learning

Abraham Maslow established Maslow's Hierarchy of Needs in 1943. Maslow's Hierarchy of Needs consists of five levels of human need. At the bottom of the hierarchy are basic human needs, including air, water, food and sleep. The top-level need is self-actualization. Every level of the hierarchy influences human behavior and motivation, including learning or how effective a person can learn.

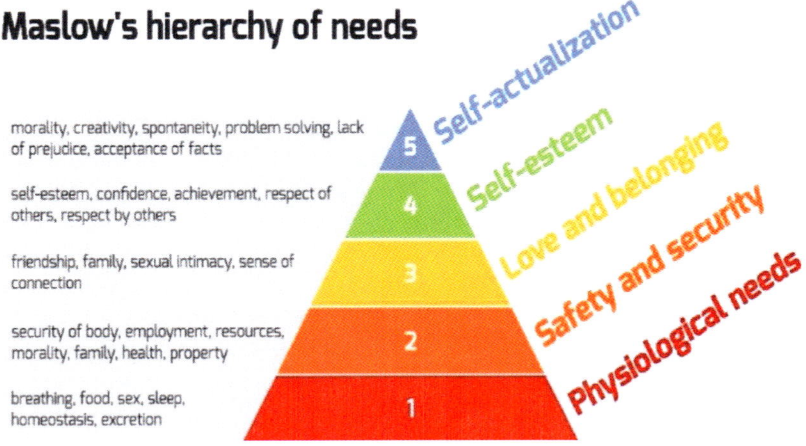

The Levels in Maslow's Hierarchy of Needs

- Physiological Needs - Air, water, food, and sleep are included in this need for a person to survive.
- Safety and Security Needs - A person needing secure, safe, and stable surroundings.
- Love and Belongingness Needs – Needs of a person to foster relationships and be part of a family and a community.
- Self-esteem Needs - Respect, self-esteem, or recognition from others.

- Self-Actualization Needs - A person wanting to reach their full potential, be creative, or develop their personal growth

Linking Maslow's Hierarchy to Learning

A. Physiological Needs and Learning

- **Impact:** Without meeting physiological needs, a student's ability to focus and engage in learning is significantly compromised. Hunger, fatigue, and poor health can severely hinder cognitive functions and information retention.

- **Application:** Ensuring that students have access to nutritious meals and adequate sleep can dramatically improve their learning outcomes. Many schools provide breakfast and lunch programs specifically designed to support these essential needs, thereby helping students remain focused and engaged in their studies.

B. Safety Needs and Learning

- **Impact:** A safe and secure environment is fundamental to effective learning. Fear, anxiety, and instability can distract students and impede their concentration, making it difficult for them to absorb and retain information.

- **Application:** Creating a safe and supportive classroom environment is crucial. This includes addressing and preventing bullying, ensuring both emotional and physical safety, and establishing consistent routines and clear rules. These measures help students feel secure and create a conducive learning atmosphere.

C. Love and Belongingness Needs and Learning

- **Impact:** Positive social interactions and a sense of belonging significantly enhance motivation and engagement in learning. Conversely, isolation and lack of social support can lead to disengagement and poor academic performance.

- **Application:** Fostering a sense of community and promoting positive relationships between students and teachers can effectively fulfill these needs. Encouraging group work, facilitating extracurricular activities, and supporting peer support groups also play an essential role in helping students feel connected and valued.

D. Esteem Needs and Learning

- **Impact:** High self-esteem and recognition from others are crucial for boosting students' confidence and motivation. On the other hand, low self-esteem can result in a lack of motivation and a heightened fear of failure.

- **Application:** Providing constructive feedback, recognizing achievements, and offering opportunities for success are vital for enhancing students' self-esteem. Setting realistic goals and celebrating progress and accomplishments further contribute to meeting esteem needs and fostering a positive learning environment.

E. Self-Actualization Needs and Learning

- **Impact:** At this level, students are driven by the desire to achieve their full potential. They engage in learning not just for academic success but for personal growth, creativity, and fulfillment.

- **Application:** Encouraging critical thinking, fostering creativity, and promoting independent learning are key to helping students reach self-actualization. Providing opportunities for exploration, innovation, and personal projects enables students to pursue their interests and develop their unique talents.

Integrating Maslow's Hierarchy in Education

A. Holistic Approach

Educators should adopt a holistic approach that considers all levels of Maslow's hierarchy. Addressing students' basic needs can create a foundation for higher-level cognitive processes and learning.

B. Support Services

Schools can offer support services such as counseling, health services, and nutritional programs to address the physiological and safety needs of students.

C. Positive Teaching and Learning Environment

Creating a positive and inclusive classroom environment where students feel valued and supported can help fulfill their love, belongingness, and esteem needs.

D. Personalized Learning

Tailoring education to meet individual students' interests and strengths can promote self-actualization and lifelong learning.

By understanding and addressing the various levels of Maslow's Hierarchy of Needs, educators can create an environment that supports their students' academic, emotional, and psychological well-being, enhancing the overall learning experience.

The Learning Pyramid

The Learning Pyramid, also known as the "Cone of Learning" or "Learning Cone," is a model that represents the effectiveness of different teaching methods on retention rates. The pyramid suggests that certain learning activities result in better retention and understanding of material. Here's how the Learning Pyramid aligns with our understanding of how the brain learns and rewires:

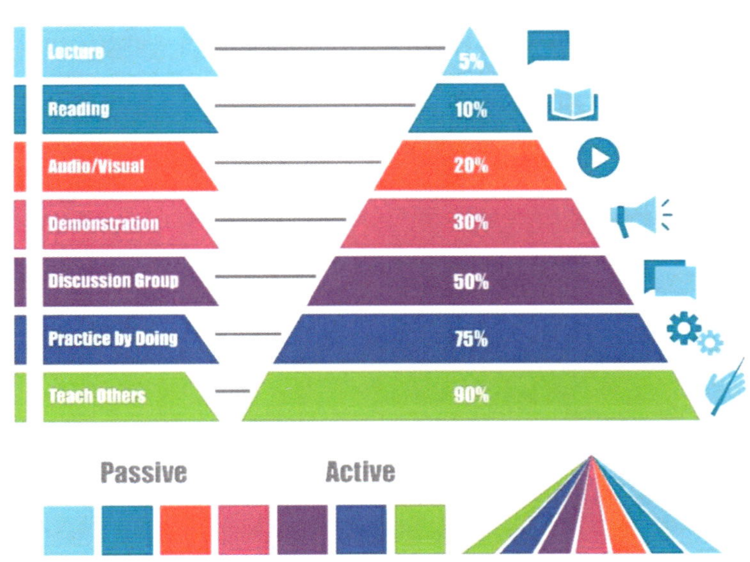

A. Passive Learning (Lower Levels of the Pyramid):

- **Lecture (5%) and Reading (10%)**
  These methods suggest lower retention rates. From a neuroplasticity perspective, passive learning involves less engagement and fewer neural connections. The brain's ability to rewire and strengthen synaptic connections is limited due to the lack of active involvement and multi-sensory engagement.

- **Audiovisual (20%) and Demonstration (30%)**
  These methods are slightly more engaging, involving more sensory input, which can aid in better retention. They provide visual and auditory stimuli that can activate different areas of the brain, leading to stronger neural connections compared to just reading or listening.

B. Active Learning (Upper Levels of the Pyramid):

- **Discussion Group (50%)**
  Engaging in discussions requires active processing, critical thinking, and verbal expression. This method stimulates various brain regions, including those responsible for language, memory, and social interaction, promoting synaptic plasticity and better retention.

- **Practice by Doing (75%)**
  Hands-on activities and practice involve motor skills, problem-solving, and real-world application, engaging multiple areas of the brain. Examples are fieldwork experience, practicum, internship, and clinical rotations. This method enhances the formation of new synaptic connections and strengthens existing ones, supporting the brain's ability to adapt and rewire through experience.

- **Teaching Others (90%)**
  The highest retention rate is achieved when learners teach others like giving tutorials to other learners. This method requires deep understanding, organization of thoughts, and communication skills. It engages the brain extensively, reinforcing neural pathways and facilitating long-term memory through repeated retrieval and articulation of knowledge.

How the Brain Changes

One of the essential changes is neuroplasticity, which refers to the brain's ability to reorganize itself by establishing new neural connections. This capacity, neuroplasticity, allows the neurons, or nerve cells, in the brain to compensate for injury and disease and to adjust their activities in response to new situations and changes in their environment.

A second essential change is synaptic plasticity, which is the brain's synaptic connections between neurons or nerve cells. The number of neurons and the strength of the synaptic connections between the neurons constantly change, which are believed to be directly associated with learning and memory. Active learning methods, which are portrayed in the upper tiers of the Learning Pyramid, result in greater synaptic plasticity because they create repeated practice and engagement, in turn creating stronger neural pathways.

A third essential change is synaptogenesis. Synaptogenesis is the activation of the formation of new connections between neurons in the brain. Synaptogenesis is essential for learning, and small activities that provide critical thinking, problem-solving, and opportunity for teaching others increase the generation of new connections and the brain's ability to store and retrieve information.

Given the principles of the Learning Pyramid, educators can develop instructional approaches to help students become engaged and retain information. For example:

- Use group discussion and collaborative projects to help students become more engaged and active learners.
- Use hands-on activities and real-world applications to help students be more engaged/active learners.
- Have students teach back the material to peers, as it reinforces their understanding and retention.

The Learning Pyramid offers a valuable perspective on the principles of brain learning and neuroplasticity. This model illustrates how various learning methods impact the brain's ability to rewire itself and form new connections. According to the Pyramid, active learning methods—those positioned higher on the Pyramid—promote greater synaptic plasticity and enhanced neural engagement. As a result, these methods lead to improved retention and understanding of the subject matter. By integrating these active learning techniques into their teaching practices, educators can significantly enhance the effectiveness of their instruction and support students in developing their cognitive abilities.

CHAPTER 3

Sleep, Brain Waves, Circadian Rhythm, and Relaxation

The Importance of Sleep for Learning and Memory

Most of us understand the importance of getting a good night's sleep, but did you know that sleep is also crucial for learning and memory? Far from being a mere luxury, sleep plays an essential role in processing and storing new information; it's a biological necessity.

In this section, we will explore why sleep is vital for the brain and its implications for learning and memory.

What Happens During Sleep?

Contrary to popular belief, your brain does not shut down when you fall asleep. It remains highly active, working diligently to process and organize the information accumulated throughout the day. One of the most critical functions of sleep is memory consolidation—a process in which short-term memories are transformed into long-term ones. During the various stages of sleep, your brain sifts through what to retain and what to discard.

Stages of Sleep

The sleep cycle encompasses several distinct stages, each playing a unique role in the processes of remembering and forgetting information:

- **Light Sleep:** This stage is fundamental for the initial processing of information. During light sleep, your brain starts to sort out and integrate the day's experiences.

- **Deep Sleep:** Also known as slow-wave sleep, this stage is crucial for consolidating both declarative memories (knowledge and facts) and procedural memories (skills and tasks). Deep sleep helps solidify new skills and information, making them more stable in your memory.
- **REM Sleep:** Rapid Eye Movement (REM) sleep is especially significant for consolidating emotional memories and integrating new information with existing knowledge. During REM sleep, the brain works on emotional processing and enhances cognitive connections, contributing to better problem-solving and creativity.

How Sleep Makes Learning Easier

A. Strengthening Neural Connections

During sleep, particularly deep sleep, your brain strengthens the synaptic connections formed during learning. This process, known as synaptic consolidation, makes it easier to retrieve memories in the future. Think of learning as creating a neural pathway; during memory consolidation, this pathway is fortified and reinforced, ensuring that the information is more easily accessible when needed.

B. Brain Cleaning

Sleep also activates the glymphatic system, which becomes more efficient while you are sleeping. This system helps clear out toxins and waste from the brain, a crucial function for maintaining optimal brain health and preventing cognitive decline. The removal of these harmful substances ensures that your brain functions at its best, supporting overall cognitive abilities.

C. Enhanced Problem-Solving Skills

Have you ever gone to bed stumped by a problem and awoken with the perfect solution? Sleep enhances problem-solving skills and creativity. During REM sleep, the brain replays and reorganizes information, strengthening connections between seemingly unrelated pieces of information. This process can lead to "aha!" moments where new insights and understandings emerge, fostering innovation and creativity.

D. Tips for Better Sleep and Learning

- **Establish a Routine:** Going to bed and waking up at the same time every day helps regulate your body's internal clock. Consistency is key to ensuring you achieve the recommended 7-9 hours of sleep per night for adults. A regular sleep schedule can significantly improve the quality of your rest and, consequently, your ability to learn and retain information.

- **Create a Relaxing Bedtime Routine:** Establishing a routine to relax and wind down before sleep can signal to your body that it's time to rest. Engaging in calming activities such as reading, taking a warm bath, or practicing meditation can prepare your body and mind for sleep, making it easier to drift off and stay asleep.

- **Screen Time Avoidance:** The blue light emitted by phones, tablets, and TVs can interfere with your ability to fall asleep. Try to avoid screens at least an hour before bedtime. If you must use a device, enable a blue light filter to minimize its impact. Reducing screen time before bed can help improve your sleep quality and overall cognitive function.

- **Create a Sleep-Friendly Environment:** Transform your bedroom into a sleep-friendly environment by maintaining a cool temperature, keeping the room dark, and minimizing noise. Investing in a good mattress and pillows can also enhance sleep quality. A comfortable and quiet sleeping space can significantly impact your ability to achieve deep, restorative sleep.

- **Ban Stimulants Late in the Day:** Caffeine and nicotine are stimulants that can make it difficult to fall asleep if consumed too close to bedtime. Try to avoid these stimulants several hours before sleep. Additionally, be cautious with alcohol; while it may initially make you feel sleepy, it can disrupt your sleep later in the night, leading to poor sleep quality.

Sleep is essential for optimizing learning and memory. It plays a vital role in calibrating new information, reinforcing neural connections, and enhancing problem-solving skills.

By adopting good sleep practices and integrating adequate sleep into your learning process, you can significantly improve your ability to remember and recall information. This, in turn, can lead to better academic performance and overall cognitive function. So, before you consider pulling an all-nighter, remember that a restful night’s sleep is one of the most effective strategies you can employ to support and enhance your brain's capabilities.

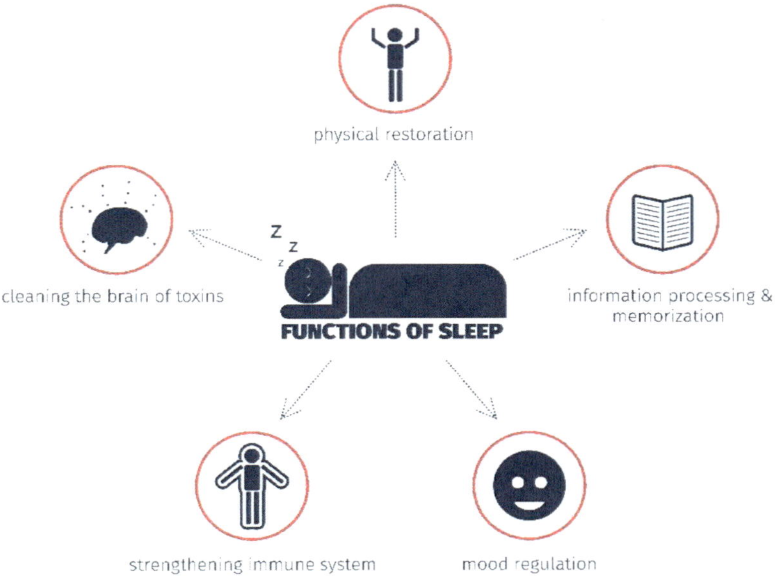

Brain Waves in Learning, Memory, and Storage

The human brain operates through electrical signals known as brain waves. These brain waves are classified by their frequency, measured in Hertz (Hz), and are associated with different levels of consciousness and cognitive processes. One Hertz equals one cycle per second. For example, if a brain wave oscillates ten times in one second, it has a frequency of 10 Hz.

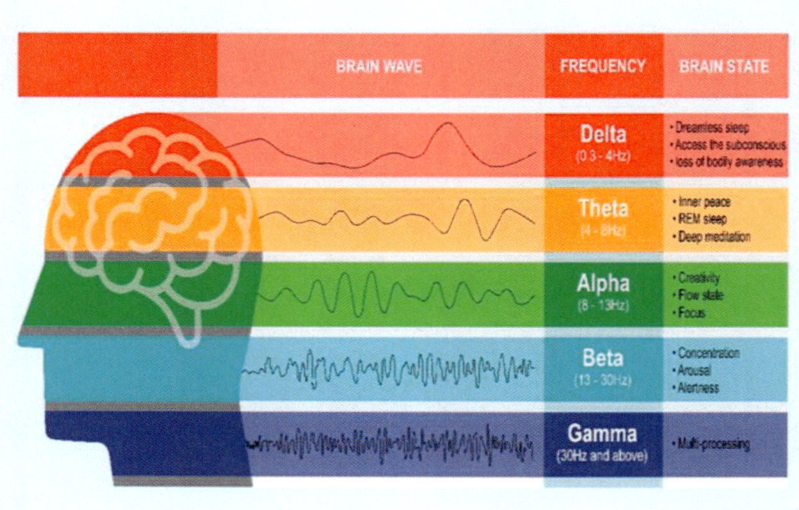

The main five categories of brain waves include:

Delta Waves (0.3 - 4 Hz)

- **State:** Deep sleep
- **Function:** Delta waves are most pronounced during deep sleep and play a crucial role in the restorative processes of sleep. While they are not heavily involved in active learning, they are essential for overall brain health and function.

Theta Waves (4 - 8 Hz)

- **State:** Light sleep, relaxation, and meditative states
- **Function:** Theta waves are active during light sleep, deep relaxation, and meditative states. They are associated with creativity and the unconscious mind. During sleep, theta waves are believed to be involved in memory consolidation and the integration of new understandings into our existing knowledge base.

Alpha Waves (8 - 13 Hz)

- **State:** Relaxed, calm, but awake state
- **Function:** Alpha waves are present when we are awake but very relaxed, such as when daydreaming or meditating. They are vital for stress reduction and are considered the optimal state for learning and memory. Alpha waves are crucial for brain coordination and promoting mental resourcefulness.

Beta Waves (13 - 30 Hz)

- **State:** Active, alert, and focused state
- **Function:** Beta waves are active during active thinking, problem-solving, and intense focus. These waves are important for conscious thought processes, decision-making, and learning new information. Beta waves are essential for acquiring, retaining, and applying new information.

Gamma Waves (30 - 100 Hz)

- **State:** High-level information processing and cognitive tasks
- **Function:** Gamma waves are involved in high cognitive functions such as attention, performance, and memory. They link information from different regions of the brain and are essential for learning, memory formation, and information storage.

To Sum it Up

- **Learning:** Beta and gamma brain waves are essential for learning, as they facilitate active engagement, attention, and the integration of new information. Beta waves help sustain focus, while gamma waves enable complex processing and coordination of information from various brain regions.

- **Memory:** Theta waves are significant in memory consolidation, particularly during sleep and REM (Rapid Eye Movement) sleep. Alpha waves support memory consolidation by creating a relaxed state conducive to processing and storing memories.
- **Storage:** Memory storage involves multiple brain wave types. Delta waves aid in deep sleep, contributing to overall brain restoration and optimizing the environment for memory storage. Theta and gamma waves work together to support memory consolidation and integration.

Understanding the roles of different brain wave types highlights the importance of maintaining a balanced mental state to optimize learning, memory formation, and cognitive functioning. Activities that promote relaxation (alpha waves) and deep sleep stages (delta and theta waves) can enhance these processes, while those that stimulate active engagement and focus (beta and gamma waves) can improve learning and memory retention.

Circadian Rhythm for Learning

The concept of a biological clock, or circadian rhythm, significantly influences the optimal times for reading, reviewing, and retaining information. This text explores how different times of the day affect these activities:

Morning (6 AM - 12 PM)

- **Cognitive Function:** Memory, attention, and executive functions are generally at their peak in the morning. Elevated cortisol levels contribute to heightened wakefulness and alertness during this period.

- **Best Activities:** Engaging in challenging cognitive tasks, such as reading complex material, learning new concepts, or solving intricate problems, can be particularly effective in the morning.

- **Memory Consolidation:** Learning new information in the morning can enhance memory retention. As the brain is fresh and more capable of processing information efficiently at this time, memory consolidation tends to be more effective.

Afternoon (12 PM - 6 PM)

- **Energy Dip:** Many individuals experience a natural dip in energy levels in the early afternoon, often referred to as the post-lunch dip. This decline can impact focus and concentration.

- **Best Activities:** During this period, it may be more beneficial to engage in less cognitively demanding tasks. Reviewing previously learned material, organizing notes, or participating in discussions may be easier and more productive.

- **Physical Activity:** Incorporating short breaks for physical activity can help counteract the afternoon energy dip and improve overall cognitive function.

Evening (6 PM - 10 PM)

- **Second Wind:** Many people experience a 'second wind' of energy in the early evening, making it an ideal time for creative activities, problem-solving, or other engaging tasks.

- **Best Activities:** This period is suitable for reviewing and summarizing information learned during the day. It is also a good time for collaborative study sessions, applying knowledge through practice problems, or working on projects.

- **Memory and Sleep:** Studying in the evening can aid in memory consolidation, as sleep plays a crucial role in retaining learned material. Reviewing material before bed can sometimes enhance retention, as the brain continues to process information during sleep.

Night (10 PM – 6 AM)

- **Sleep:** Sleep is essential for memory functions and overall cognitive abilities. Insufficient or poor-quality sleep can negatively impact learning and memory.

- **Optimal Activities:** To promote effective sleep, maintain good sleep hygiene by turning off electronics and engaging in less stimulating activities before bed. Light reading or listening to relaxing music can help transition your body into sleep mode.

Understanding your individual chronotype—whether you are a morning lark or a night owl—is crucial for effectively scheduling learning activities. Recognizing your chronotype allows you to plan your study schedule in alignment with your natural rhythms.

Experimenting with different times of the day for studying can help you identify your optimal study periods. Keeping a log of your study activities and interactions can also reveal your learning patterns and preferences.

By becoming more aware of your body's natural working clock and aligning your study activities with your peak cognitive performance times, you can enhance learning, memory, recall, and overall academic performance. Implementing study strategies such as taking regular breaks, maintaining good sleep hygiene, and acknowledging your personal chronotype can lead to more efficient and effective studying.

Relaxation Strategies

Effective learning is a nuanced blend of focus, hard work, stress management, and relaxation. To concentrate and manage stress effectively, a relaxed and clear mind is essential. The following relaxation strategies can enhance your learning:

A. Deep Breathing Exercises Strategy

Utilize deep breathing to activate the parasympathetic nervous system, promoting relaxation. Inhale deeply through the nose, allowing your breath to be slow and steady. Pause for a few seconds, then exhale slowly and controlled through the mouth.

Benefits: Deep breathing helps reduce stress and anxiety, enhances concentration, and improves focus. It also lowers heart rate and blood pressure, creating an optimal state for learning.

B. Progressive Muscle Relaxation (PMR) Strategy

Systematically tense and then relax different muscle groups in your body, starting from your toes and working up to your head. Experience the contrast between tension and relaxation.

Benefits: PMR alleviates physical tension from prolonged sitting during study sessions, promotes overall relaxation, and may enhance sleep quality—an important factor in memory consolidation.

C. Mindfulness Meditation Strategy
Find a quiet place to sit and focus on your breath. When your mind wanders, gently redirect your attention back to your breathing. You might use guided meditation apps like Headspace or Calm.

Benefits: Mindfulness meditation improves attention, reduces cognitive fatigue, enhances emotional regulation, and decreases stress, leading to greater focus during studying.

D. Visualization Strategy
Close your eyes and imagine a calming scene, such as a beach or forest. Engage all your senses to fully immerse yourself in this mental escape.

Benefits: Visualization helps reduce anxiety by providing a mental retreat. It is particularly useful for calming nerves before exams or presentations and for boosting confidence.

E. Yoga & Stretch Strategy
Incorporate gentle yoga postures and stretching into your daily routine. Focus on poses that promote relaxation and flexibility, such as Child's Pose or Forward Fold.

Benefits: Enhancing circulation and reducing physical tension through yoga and stretching can boost cognitive functioning. These practices combine physical activity with conscious breathing to alleviate stress and enhance overall well-being.

F. Music Therapy
Listen to calming music while studying or during breaks. Create a playlist of soothing tunes that foster a tranquil study environment.

Benefits: Music has the power to reduce anxiety and stress, thereby improving concentration. It also provides an emotional backdrop that can make learning experiences more enjoyable.

G. Time Management and Breaks
Employ the Pomodoro Technique (25 minutes of studying, followed by a 5-minute break; repeat this cycle four times, then take a longer break). Incorporate regular breaks to stand, move, or walk around.

Benefits: This technique supports sustained attention and productivity by balancing focused activity with periodic relaxation. It allows the brain to rest and process information more effectively, leading to better retention.

H. Lifestyle Choices
Adopt a balanced approach to nutrition, sleep, and hydration across all areas of your life. Regular exercise also supports cognitive processing, focus, and stress reduction.

Benefits: A healthy body contributes to a healthy mind, enhancing cognitive functioning and learning abilities while minimizing stress.

Incorporating these relaxation and enhancement strategies into your daily routine can have lasting positive effects on your learning. Managing stress effectively enables you to improve retention and maintain a calm, focused mind. Prioritize both your physical and mental health to enhance your overall learning experience.

CHAPTER 4

Attention, Learning, Memory and Consolidation

In a world exploding with information, we are moving at an ever-increasing speed. To keep up, our ability to learn and remember becomes critical. When we discuss cognitive processes and strategies that support learning, we must consider several broad functions: attention, learning, memory, and consolidation.

In educational settings, especially during lectures, the concept of attention span is essential to consider. Studies indicate that students begin to lose their focus after approximately 20 to 30 minutes of a continuous lecture. To combat this decline in attention, it is beneficial to incorporate interactive components, breaks, and other engaging variables. One effective approach is active learning, where students participate in meaningful activities such as discussions, group projects, or problem-solving tasks, which help sustain their attention spans.

Factors Affecting Attention Span

A. Age

Typically, children have shorter attention spans than. For instance, very young children aged 2 to 5 may focus for only 5 to 10 minutes, while older children aged 6 to 10 years might maintain focus for 20 to 30 minutes. In contrast, adults generally possess longer attention spans; however, this can vary significantly depending on the individual and the task at hand.

B. Task Engagement

The nature of the task significantly influences attention span. Tasks that are personally meaningful or stimulating tend to capture and maintain attention more than those that are monotonous or uninteresting. Engaging students with relevant content can enhance their focus and retention.

C. Environmental Influences

Environmental factors play a crucial role in shaping span. Distractions such as noise, interruptions, or uncomfortable settings can hinder one's ability to concentrate. Conversely, quiet, comfortable, and organized environments are more conducive to favorable focus, allowing individuals to immerse themselves in the learning experience.

D. Mental and Physical Health

Both mental and physical health substantially impact attention spans. For example, individuals with Attention Deficit Hyperactivity Disorder (ADHD) may experience significant challenges in maintaining focus. Additionally, mental fatigue, stress, and lack of sleep can severely compromise one’s ability to concentrate, further diminishing attention spans.

Learning Strategies

Learning can become more efficient and enjoyable by applying appropriate techniques. The following practical tips focus on helping you improve your attention and focus while enhancing your memory and retention.

A. Minimize Distractions

Begin by creating a workspace with minimal distractions. Put your phone on silent, choose a space where you can have uninterrupted time, and inform others that you are dedicating time to yourself. It’s remarkable how much work you can accomplish when you’re not being pulled in multiple directions. For example, when preparing for an exam, activate airplane mode on your phone and find a quiet area in your home or a secluded corner of the library. This simple step can significantly enhance your productivity.

B. Break It Down

Instead of attempting to tackle everything at once, segment your study times into smaller, manageable parts. One effective technique is the Pomodoro Technique: study for 25 minutes, then take a 5-minute break. After completing four cycles, take a longer break. This method not only helps maintain focus but also prevents burnout. For instance, if you plan to study for two hours, you can divide your time into four 25-minute segments, allowing for brief breaks in between to recharge.

C. Stay Organized

Keep your study area and materials well organized. An uncluttered space can help you feel more in control and less stressed, making it easier to focus. Utilize a planner or organizational apps to track assignments and deadlines, which can help you stay on top of your responsibilities.

D. Set Clear Goals

Before you begin studying, identify clear objectives and determine what you want to achieve during your session. Specificity in your approach is vital, as it provides a framework that makes it easier to concentrate. For instance, when studying history, decide to delve deeply into a specific chapter or, even better, choose to memorize key dates and facts relevant to that day's material. This focused approach can enhance your retention and understanding.

E. Meditate or Be Mindful

Mindfulness practices can significantly improve your focus over time. Taking a few moments to engage in simple mindfulness exercises, such as short meditation or deep breathing techniques, can help calm your mind and keep you centered on the task at hand.

Ultimately, dedicating time to these practices can distinguish between a productive study session and one that is unfocused. For example, consider taking five minutes to perform deep breathing exercises or participate in a guided meditation before diving into your study materials. This can prepare your mind for optimal focus.

Enhancing Memory and Retention

A. Mnemonics

Mnemonics are powerful memory strategies that can assist you in recalling important information. These can take various forms, from acronyms to vivid visual images. For example, to remember the order of the planets, you might use the acronym: "My Very Educated Mother Just Served Us Noodles," which represents Mercury, Venus, Earth, Mars, Jupiter, Saturn, Uranus, and Neptune. Similarly, to remember the Great Lakes, you can use the acronym "HOMES," which stands for Huron, Ontario, Michigan, Erie, and Superior. Utilizing such techniques can make memorization more engaging and effective.

B. Teach What You Learned

One of the most effective ways to reinforce new material is to teach it to someone else. Summarizing and explaining what you've learned solidifies your understanding and highlights areas that may need further clarification. For instance, after reading a chapter on cellular biology, try teaching the process of mitosis to a friend, family member, or even your pet. This method not only reinforces your knowledge but also enhances your communication skills.

C. Using Multiple Senses

Engaging multiple senses can strengthen memory retention. Read the material aloud, write it down, draw diagrams, or even create physical models. The more senses you involve in your academic work, the stronger the memories that are formed. For example, when studying anatomy, use colored markers to highlight different body systems while vocalizing the names out loud. This multisensory approach can enhance your learning experience.

D. Practice Spaced Repetition

Instead of cramming all at once, spread your study sessions over time. Spaced repetition involves increasing the intervals between review sessions as time progresses. This technique is effective in transitioning information from short-term to long-term memory, increasing the likelihood of retaining the information later. For instance, when studying vocabulary for a language class, review the new words on the day you learn them, then again the following day, and continue this pattern weekly.

E. Get Plenty of Sleep

Sleep is critical for memory consolidation. Ensure you are getting enough rest, particularly around exam periods. A good night's sleep allows your brain to process and store information effectively. For example, if you are studying hard for an exam, aim for seven hours of sleep instead of sacrificing rest for last-minute cramming. Prioritizing sleep can significantly improve your performance.

F. Stay Hydrated and Eat Well

Your diet and hydration levels can greatly affect your memory and cognitive function. Stay hydrated and consume a balanced diet rich in nutrients that promote brain health. Foods such as fish, nuts, berries, and leafy greens support cognitive function and enhance memory. For example, consider snacking on walnuts and blueberries during your study breaks to keep your brain energized.

G. Use Visual Aids

Visual aids can significantly enhance your ability to remember information. Charts, graphs, and mind maps allow you to see information in a more digestible format. Engaging with the subject from different perspectives through visuals can aid retention. For instance, when studying the water cycle, you might create a detailed chart illustrating each stage, using arrows to trace the movement of water throughout the cycle.

H. Connect New Material to What You Already Know

Linking new information to existing knowledge can make it easier to remember. For example, if you're learning about a new concept in science, try to relate it to a personal experience or something you already understand. If you are studying physics, consider how the material relates to sports you play or common activities, such as driving a car. Making these connections deepens your understanding and recall.

I. Take Intervals

Taking breaks during study sessions helps you avoid mental fatigue. Step away, stretch, go for a walk, or engage in an enjoyable activity. Short breaks can refresh your mental energy, allowing you to return to your studies with renewed focus. For example, after an hour of studying, take a 10–15-minute break to stretch, grab a snack, or chat with a friend.

J. Engagement and Application

- **Hands-On Learning:** The most effective way to reinforce learning is to apply the information multiple times. This can be through practice exercises, real-world applications, or even teaching someone else. By actively engaging with the material, you reinforce your learning and contextualize the information.

- **Simulate and Play:** If you're acquiring a new skill, try creating simulations of situations where you would apply that skill. For example, in language learning, role-playing conversations can be an incredibly effective way to practice and gain confidence.

- **Strategize and Reflect:** Cultivate self-awareness through reflection on your learning experiences. Consider which strategies are effective, which are not, and how you could improve. This reflective practice can help you become a more effective learner, continuously refining your approach to studying.

Consolidation of Learning Across Lessons

Consolidation of learning across lessons is a crucial step in the learning process. It involves reviewing, synthesizing, and reinforcing the content covered throughout the course to ensure a deep understanding and long-term retention. Below is an expansion on how to effectively engage in consolidating learning:

A. Review Key Concepts and Recap Each Lesson

Refresh Each Lesson: Quickly revisit the key points from each lesson to refresh your memory. This includes revisiting definitions, theories, and methods discussed in the lesson content. Utilize summaries provided by the instructor or develop your own concise summaries for each topic. This practice helps reinforce the essential concepts and enhances recall.

- **Active Recall:** Practice retrieving information without looking at your notes. This method can significantly enhance recall and reinforce learning. Use flashcards or quiz yourself with questions that target the key points from each lesson. For instance, consider creating a quiz that challenges you to explain major concepts from the last few lessons without referring to your materials.

B. Interactive Discussions

- **Group Discussions:** Participate in discussions with fellow students to deepen your understanding. The act of explaining concepts to others can clarify your comprehension and highlight any gaps in your knowledge. Organize study groups where each member is responsible for reviewing one lesson and teaching it to the rest of the group. This collaborative approach not only reinforces learning but also fosters a supportive learning environment.

- **Q&A Sessions:** Arrange Q&A sessions for students to ask questions and clarify doubts. These interactions can provide new perspectives and deepen understanding. Encourage students to pose questions and engage in discussions on forums or online platforms. This not only facilitates learning but also creates a sense of community among students.

C. Practical Application

- **Real-World Situations:** Apply theoretical concepts to actual scenarios. This method of contextual learning makes abstract ideas more tangible and memorable. Utilize case studies or problem-solving tasks that relate directly to the course content. For example, analyzing real-world case studies in business courses can enhance your ability to connect theory with practice.

- **Projects and Presentations:** Engage in individual or group projects or give presentations that span multiple lessons. This can assist in synthesizing course content and promote a broader understanding. Create visual aids, such as posters or slide shows, to illustrate the main concepts and how they interconnect, making your presentations more engaging and informative.

D. Reflection and Metacognition

- **Reflective Journaling:** Regularly write reflections on what you have learned, how you have applied the information, and how your understanding has evolved over time. This practice strengthens self-awareness and metacognition. Journaling can also help identify strengths and areas needing further review. For instance, you might reflect on what strategies worked well for you in your last study session and what changes could enhance your learning.

- **Goal Setting:** Determine what you want to achieve from your learning experience and set specific, measurable goals. For example, aim to master particular concepts or apply new skills in different scenarios. Regularly review and adjust your goals based on your progress and emerging learning needs. This dynamic approach ensures that your learning remains focused and relevant.

E. Assessment and Feedback

- **Formative Assessment:** Complete practice tests or quizzes to assess your understanding of topics from all lessons. These practice questions can help identify areas where you need to concentrate your review and gauge your overall understanding of the material. Utilize a variety of question types, such as multiple-choice, short answer, and essay questions, to target different skills and aspects of your knowledge.

- **Seek Feedback:** Request feedback from an instructor or peers regarding your comprehension and performance. Constructive feedback can provide positive reinforcement for your strengths while offering direction for improvement. Reflect on the feedback you receive and adjust your study strategies accordingly to optimize your learning.

F. Review Sessions:

- **Scheduled Review:** Plan regular review sessions as you approach exams or assessments. Space out these sessions to minimize the likelihood of forgetting material. Cover different topics in each review session to provide a comprehensive overview and reinforce your learning.

- **Consolidated Notes:** Create a single document that combines notes from different lessons to better understand the connections between them. This document can serve as a comprehensive review resource. Employ effective note-taking strategies, such as color coding and mind mapping, to highlight key points and illustrate relationships between different concepts.

These strategies can help students consolidate their learning so that they do not merely know or understand the material but also retain it and apply what they have learned. By utilizing a comprehensive approach, we can support students in their ability to consolidate learning, ensure long-term success in their academic careers, and foster a deeper understanding of their chosen subject areas.

CHAPTER 5

Cramming, Test Anxiety, Note-Taking, and Reviewing

The Dangers of Cramming: Cognitive Overload

Cramming is a method of studying in which students intensely review information shortly before an examination. While this technique aims to help students remember material in a short period, it often proves ineffective as a regular studying strategy. For many, frequent cramming can lead to mental blocks, undermining overall academic performance.

A. Mental Block

The pressure of an impending exam, combined with the stress of cramming, can result in a mental block. This phenomenon occurs when your mind goes blank, rendering you unable to recall any of the information you studied. Mental blocks are closely linked to high anxiety levels, which disrupt the neural processes involved in memory retrieval.

B. Overloading Working Memory

Working memory is responsible for holding and processing information in the short term. During a cramming session, students often overwhelm their working memory by cramming in too much information at once. However, working memory has a limited capacity. When overloaded, it becomes increasingly difficult to function effectively, which negatively impacts cognitive performance during the exam. A less efficient memory retrieval process will hinder your ability to recall the necessary information.

C. Lack of Proper Encoding

Encoding is the process of converting information into a form that can be stored in long-term memory. Effective encoding requires time and repeated exposure to the material. Unfortunately, cramming does not allow sufficient time for this crucial process, leading to superficial encoding and diminished retention of information.

D. Increased Stress Levels and Anxiety

Cramming typically results in heightened stress and anxiety, as students strive to absorb vast amounts of information in a limited timeframe. Elevated levels of stress hormones, such as cortisol, can impair cognitive functions like memory retrieval and concentration, making it more challenging to recall information during the exam.

E. Sleep and Its Effects

- **Lack of Sleep:** When students engage in cramming, they often sacrifice sleep, studying late into the night or even pulling all-nighters. Insufficient sleep can leave students extremely fatigued, potentially leading to forgetfulness regarding what they studied. Adequate sleep is essential for memory consolidation and allows the brain to process newly acquired information. Without sufficient rest before an exam, students risk decreased cognitive function and may experience mental blocks during the test.

- **Reduced Cognitive Function:** Insufficient sleep can adversely affect various cognitive functions, including attention, decision-making, and problem-solving. These impairments can make it difficult to focus during an exam, understand questions, and accurately recall information.

F. Ineffective Study Techniques

- **Lack of Practice and Revision:** Effective studying involves spaced repetition and periodic self-testing, which are crucial for consolidating knowledge. Cramming neglects these essential components, resulting in poorly consolidated information. Regular practice and revision strengthen neuronal connections in the brain, making it easier to remember information during exams.

- **Shallow Processing:** Students frequently resort to memorization when cramming, a technique that constitutes shallow processing. This approach focuses solely on rehearsing information rather than fostering a deep understanding of the material. To facilitate long-term retention and retrieval, students should engage in deeper processing by making meaningful connections with the information.

Strategies to Prevent Cramming

To help you avoid the negative effects of cramming and enhance your exam results, consider utilizing the following effective study strategies:

A. Spaced Repetition

Space out your study sessions instead of cramming the night before. This approach aids in better encoding and retention of information, allowing for more effective long-term memory storage.

B. Active Learning

Engage in activities that require you to interact with the material. This can include summarizing information, teaching others, or applying concepts to different scenarios.

C. Practice Tests

Conduct practice tests to simulate exam conditions. This not only exposes you to the material multiple times but also enhances your retrieval skills, making it easier to recall information during actual exams.

D. Healthy Lifestyle

Prioritize adequate sleep, nutritious meals, and regular exercise. These habits ensure that your brain functions at its best, contributing to optimal cognitive performance.

E. Stress Management

Incorporate relaxation techniques such as deep breathing, meditation, or yoga to reduce anxiety and improve your focus. Managing stress effectively can significantly enhance your ability to study and retain information.

By understanding the detrimental effects of cramming on your learning and implementing these strategies, you can improve your study habits, reduce exam-related stress, and increase your chances of achieving academic success

Dealing with Test Anxiety

Managing test anxiety can be a daunting task for many students. However, understanding the mechanisms of your brain and applying your knowledge of neuroplasticity to develop effective strategies can make this challenge less intimidating. With that in mind, let's put the tips for managing test anxiety into practice:

A. Understand and Acknowledge Anxiety Awareness

Recognizing that test anxiety is common and normal is the first step in managing it. Acknowledge your feelings and understand that test anxiety activates the fight-or-flight response, which can impair concentration and memory.

B. Use Cognitive Strategies

- **Visualization:** Try visualization techniques by imagining the entire process of taking your test and succeeding. Engaging in this practice can create neural pathways that foster feelings of confidence and success.

- **Cognitive Restructuring:** Replace negative thoughts, such as “I will fail this test,” with positive affirmations like, “I feel prepared, and I will do my best.” This evidence-based practice is successfully employed in cognitive-behavioral therapy (CBT) to rewire negative thinking.

C. Practice Effective Study Techniques

- **Spaced Repetition**: Utilize spaced repetition study techniques that gradually increase the review of material your are learning or have learned in class. This approach helps your brain efficiently recall information by leveraging neuroplasticity and the natural learning process.

- **Active Learning:** Engage in active learning strategies to better understand the material. Methods such as rephrasing concepts in your own words, explaining the information to someone else, or using flashcards can strengthen the connections in your brain.

D. Incorporate Physical Activity

Regular physical activity has been shown to reduce anxiety by increasing the production of endorphins and neurotrophic factors that support brain health and neuroplasticity. The calming effects of activities like walking, running, or even yoga can be particularly helpful before a test if you find yourself feeling anxious.

E. Leverage Mindfulness and Relaxation Techniques

- **Mindfulness Meditation:** Practicing mindfulness meditation has been shown to decrease stress and anxiety, helping to rewire your brain to respond to stress more calmly. Techniques such as deep breathing, progressive muscle relaxation, and guided imagery can effectively alleviate stress.

- **Relaxation Techniques:** Diaphragmatic breathing exercises and progressive muscle relaxation can serve as valuable strategies before your test to calm your mind and body. This approach reduces stress levels by engaging the parasympathetic nervous system.

E. Study Smarter, Not Harder

- Structured Plan of Attack: Break down your study materials into smaller parts and create a realistic study plan. This can help prevent the last-minute cyclical behavior and stress that often accompany procrastination.

- **Set Goals:** Establish specific, realistic study goals for each session. This practice can enhance your focus and keep you on track.

G. Get Enough Sleep

- **Sleep Hygiene:** Aim to get 7-9 hours of sleep per night, as sleep is one of the most important factors in memory consolidation and cognitive function. A well-rested brain can better understand and retain the information you are learning.

- **Maintain a Consistent Sleep Schedule:** Try to keep a regular sleep cycle, even on weekends. This consistency can help calibrate your body's internal clock and improve the quality of your sleep.

H. Seek Support

- **Just Talking About It:** Don't underestimate the value of talking with friends or a counselor. Sometimes, sharing your worries can help alleviate stress and anxiety.

- **Join or Create a Study Group:** Studying with peers can provide support and make you feel less isolated while promoting a more comprehensive engagement with the material.

I. Healthy Choices

- **Dietary Suggestions:** Follow a healthy, balanced diet to ensure your brain receives the necessary nutrients. Avoid excessive caffeine and sugary foods that can trigger anxiety.

- **Stay Hydrated:** Keep yourself hydrated. Dehydration can negatively impact cognitive functioning and increase feelings of stress and anxiety.

J. Exam Practice

Take practice exams under conditions similar to the actual test. This can help reduce anxiety by making the exam environment feel more familiar.

By understanding your brain and implementing these strategies, you can effectively manage test anxiety and ultimately improve your performance. The strategies above directly impact your body's stress response systems.

Psycho-Behavioral Strategies and Their Benefits

A. Deep Breathing Exercises

- **Action:** The parasympathetic nervous system is activated through deep breathing, counterbalancing the stress-induced activation of the sympathetic nervous system (fight-or-flight response), thereby reducing heart rate and blood pressure.

- **Strategy:** Try the 4-7-8 breathing technique: Inhale deeply through your nose for 4 seconds, hold your breath for 7 seconds, and exhale slowly through your mouth for 8 seconds. Repeat this several times until you feel calmer.

B. Progressive Muscle Relaxation (PMR)

- **Action:** The PMR technique involves tensing and then relaxing different muscle groups in the body, resulting in reduced physical tension and overall relaxation, which can help decrease stress and anxiety symptoms.

- **Strategy:** Begin at your toes and work your way up to your head. Tense each muscle group for about 5 seconds and then release for 20 seconds, paying attention to the sensations between tension and relaxation.

C. Regular Physical Exercise

- **Action:** Exercise boosts endorphin production, the body's natural mood lifters, and lowers stress hormone levels, such as cortisol and adrenaline. Over time, regular exercise can improve sleep, increase energy, and generally enhance your mood.

- **Strategy:** Aim for at least 30 minutes of moderate exercise most days of the week. Activities such as walking, dancing, swimming, running, or yoga can be particularly beneficial.

D. Adequate Sleep

- **Action:** Sufficient sleep plays a fundamental role in brain function, including memory consolidation and emotional regulation. Lack of sleep can exacerbate anxiety symptoms and impair cognitive function.

- **Strategy:** Aim to get 7-9 hours of sleep per night. Establish a regular sleep routine by going to bed and waking up at the same time each day, even on weekends. Make your bedroom cool, dark, and quiet, and avoid screens before bedtime.

E. Mindfulness and Meditation

- **Process:** Mindfulness and meditation practices enhance activity in the prefrontal cortex, which regulates emotions, and reduce activity in the amygdala, responsible for fear responses. Ultimately, these practices lead to decreased anxiety and improved emotional control.

- **Practice:** Set aside time each day for mindfulness or meditation. Find a comfortable place to sit, focus on your breathing, and gently bring your attention back to your breath whenever your mind wanders. Mobile apps like Headspace or Calm can guide you in mindfulness exercises.

F. Healthy Diet

- **Process:** Proper nutrition supports overall brain health and stabilizes blood sugar levels, positively affecting mood and energy levels. Certain foods, such as those containing omega-3 fatty acids, antioxidants, or magnesium, can help reduce anxiety.

- **Practice:** Eat a healthy diet rich in fruits and vegetables, lean proteins, and whole grains. Monitor your intake of caffeine and sugar, as they can elevate anxiety levels. Ensure you stay hydrated throughout the day.

G. Biofeedback

- **Process:** Biofeedback is a technique in which sensors provide real-time feedback on physiological functions such as heart rate, muscle tension, or skin temperature. By learning to control these functions, individuals can alleviate physical symptoms of anxiety.

- **Practice:** Under the guidance of a trained biofeedback therapist, learn how to manage your stress response and apply this knowledge during high-stress situations, such as before a test.

H. Consistent Study Habits

- **Process:** Establishing a consistent study routine reduces the urge to cram information right before a test. Consistent study habits reinforce learning and increase memory retention, ultimately leading to greater confidence.

- **Practice:** Research suggests dividing your study time into shorter periods separated by breaks. Use strategies such as spaced repetition to review material over time, and conduct practice exams under similar conditions to increase familiarity and decrease anxiety on the day of the actual test.

By incorporating these psychological strategies into your test preparation, you can mitigate the effects of test anxiety and enhance your overall performance. Rather than merely addressing the symptoms of test anxiety, these strategies contribute to a long-term sense of resilience and well-being.

Effective Notetaking

Taking notes is an essential skill for effective learning and academic success. It aids in retention and understanding, supports exam preparation, and enhances overall learning. This guide explains the importance of taking notes and provides strategies for effective note-taking.

Why Taking Notes is Important

Taking notes helps encode information into your memory. The act of writing things down reinforces your memory during study sessions. This process encourages you to listen actively and engage with lectures, thereby increasing your comprehension and retention.

A. Organizes Information

Taking notes structure information in a coherent format, making it easier to review and study later. Well-organized notes can serve as invaluable study resources during exam preparation.

B. Enhances Focus and Attention

Taking notes keeps you actively engaged by requiring you to pay attention to the presented material. It helps you focus and minimize distractions during lectures or study sessions.

C. Aids in Exam Preparation
Comprehensive notes can serve as reliable study guides for exams. They help identify key concepts and essential information needed for success.

How to Take Effective Notes
A. Choose the Right Method:

- **Cornell Method:** Divide your page into three sections (notes, cues, and summary). Take notes in the main section, jot down keywords or questions in the left-hand section, and write a summary at the bottom.

- **Outlining Method:** Organize information hierarchically using headings and subheadings. This method works well for structured subjects.

- **Mapping Method:** Create visual representations of the information through diagrams or mind maps. This method is particularly effective for visual learners.

B. Engage and Discern
Stay engaged while listening and aim to understand the material rather than taking detailed dictation. Recognize the main arguments, theses, and important details. Use bullet points, headers, and sub-headers to structure your notes effectively.

C. Make Use of Abbreviations and Symbols
Develop a system of abbreviations and symbols that saves time and effort. For example, you might abbreviate "and" as "&," "leads to" as "→," and "with" as "w/." Ensure that your abbreviations are consistent and meaningful when you review them later.

D. Revamp and Revise

Review your notes to reinforce your learning and fill in any gaps. Summarize the major points and add any additional information you missed during the lecture. Revise your original notes to enhance clarity and organization. Highlight or underline important items in color to draw attention to them.

E. Incorporate Visuals

Integrate diagrams, charts, and other visuals to represent complex concepts and relationships more clearly. Visuals enhance communication of the material and make your notes more engaging.

F. Keep Organized

Organize your notes by date, topic, and subject. Use dividers or folders to separate different subjects or modules. Note-taking apps like OneNote, Evernote, or Google Keep can help you maintain organization and easily locate your notes.

Note-taking is a skill that enhances your learning and academic performance. Developing effective note-taking habits will improve your retention of material, prepare you better for exams, and contribute to a successful academic year.

Reviewing After Class

Reviewing after class fosters better retention, deeper understanding, reduced stress, and enhanced cognitive function—factors that collectively contribute to improved academic performance. In contrast, cramming is less effective and can lead to increased anxiety and poorer exam results. By adopting a habit of regular review, students can optimize their learning and achieve greater success in their studies.

Effective review of notes, class lectures, and textbooks is crucial for solidifying learning and retaining information. Here are some strategies to maximize your time spent reviewing and studying:

A. Immediate Review

- **Short Review:** After class, spend 5 to 10 minutes casually reviewing your notes. This reinforces the material while it is still fresh in your memory.

- **Clarify Any Misunderstandings:** Identify unclear ideas and clarify them by consulting the textbook, a classmate, or the instructor.

B. Organize Your Notes

- **Rewrite and Organize Your Notes:** Take time to rewrite and organize your notes in a clearer format or summarize key concepts. This approach exposes you to the material in different ways, creating multiple pathways for information retention.

- **Highlight Important Ideas:** Utilize highlighters or different colored pens to emphasize key concepts, definitions, or examples.

C. Creating Study Aids

- **Flashcards:** Utilize flashcards for definitions and concepts. An app like Anki is beneficial because it creates digital cards with spaced repetition, a well-known memory technique.

- **Mind Maps:** Construct mind maps to visualize ideas. This technique can be particularly useful for understanding complex concepts and aiding retention.

D. Active Recall and Practice

- **Self-Testing:** Engage in self-testing by verbalizing the material, completing quizzes, or solving problems. Active recall is essential for reinforcing memory and learning.

- **Teach Others:** Try explaining the material to a friend or speaking it aloud. This method helps organize your thoughts and may reveal areas of misunderstanding. Teaching the material allows you to identify gaps in your knowledge.

E. Integrate Readings and Textbooks

- **Combine Notes and Readings:** Integrate your lecture notes with your textbook. This combination offers different perspectives and leads to a more comprehensive understanding of the concepts being studied.

- **Utilize Additional Materials:** Incorporate supplementary resources, such as online articles, videos, or academic journals. These materials can deepen your understanding of the topics.

F. Regular Review Sessions

- **Spaced Repetition:** Implement a schedule of regular reviews at spaced intervals (e.g., one day, one week, one month) for long-term retention.

- **Weekly Reviews:** Designate time each week to review your notes and course materials.

G. Be Active During Studying

- **Ask Questions:** As you review, pose questions about the material. Why is this concept important? How does it connect to other concepts or themes you've learned?

- **Apply the Material:** Consider real-life examples of how you could apply the concepts. This application leads to a deeper understanding and enhanced retention.

H. Tech Options

- **Digital Notes:** Maintain digital notes that sync across devices. Apps like Evernote or OneNote can be particularly useful. Digital notes can also incorporate hyperlinks, images, and other multimedia to make learning more engaging.

- **Educational Resources:** Explore various online resources, such as Quizlet for flashcards, Khan Academy for supplemental learning, and numerous Massive Open Online Course (MOOC) platforms for additional practice and resources.

Example of a Review Session

A. Review and Rewrite (10-15 minutes)

Look over any notes you took during class. Rewrite or summarize the main points in your own words.

B. Create Flashcards or Study Aids (20-30 minutes)

Create flashcards for key terms or concepts. Alternatively, develop a mind map that connects the big ideas together.

C. Active Recall and Practice Questions (15-20 minutes)

Test yourself using flashcards. Try answering practice questions from your textbook or online resources.

D. Weekly Review (30-60 minutes)

Review your notes and the flashcards from the week. Make a quick summary of the week's lessons and link them to what you learned in previous weeks.

Length of Review After Class

The amount of time necessary for review after class depends on various factors, such as the content's difficulty, the learner's familiarity with the subject matter, and personal learning preferences. However, educational studies suggest some general principles and recommendations for review duration.

A. Review Immediately (10-15 minutes)

A quick review right after class provides an opportunity to reinforce learning and clarify any confusion while the information is still fresh in your mind.

B. Daily Review (30-60 minutes)

Devoting at least 30 minutes to an hour each day to reviewing notes and materials can further strengthen understanding and boost retention. For more complex subjects, two hours of review with breaks in between is recommended.

C. Weekly Review (2-3 hours)

Conducting an in-depth review once a week can be beneficial for reinforcing the content covered during the week and connecting new information to previously learned material. For more difficult subjects, four hours of review with breaks in between is suggested.

Factors Impacting Review Time

A. Difficulty of the Content

More challenging topics or those that are new or unfamiliar to the learner may require more time for review compared to simpler subjects or those that the learner is already familiar with.

B. Learning Preferences

Individual learning preferences play a crucial role in review time. Some learners may need more frequent review sessions and repetition to effectively remember and retain information, while others may require less. Understanding one's learning style can help determine the optimal amount of review time necessary for effective learning.

C. Frequency of Review

The likelihood of retaining information often depends on how frequently one engages with the material after the initial study session. Research on learning underscores the benefits of spaced review; that is, recalling and revisiting material over time. Generally, reviewing the material in shorter sessions more frequently is more effective than longer, less frequent study sessions.

CHAPTER 6

Neuroplasticity:

The Brain's Ability to Adapt

The human brain is highly adaptable, continually reorganizing itself throughout our lives. This remarkable ability is known as neuroplasticity. In this chapter, we will explore what neuroplasticity is and how it can be harnessed to enhance brain function.

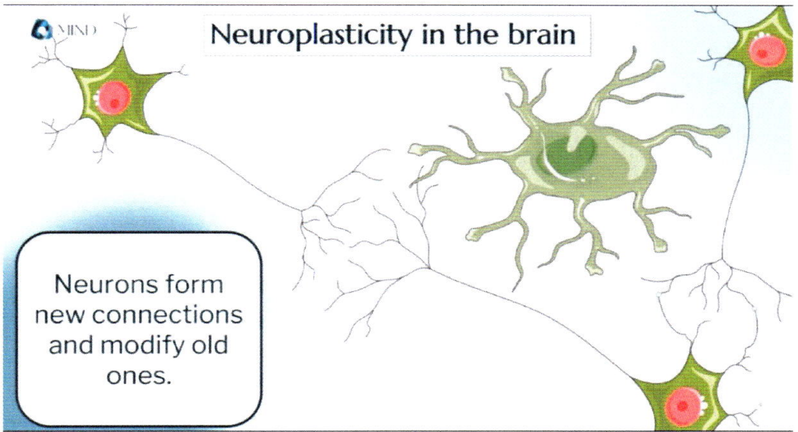

An Overview of Neuroplasticity

A. Define Neuroplasticity

Neuroplasticity can be likened to a makeover for the brain. It describes the brain's capacity to form new neural connections and pathways, or to modify existing ones, in response to learning, experience, or injury. This process is similar to updating software on our mobile phones or computers—just as these devices need updates to remain efficient, our brains require neuroplasticity to stay up-to-date and effective.

B. How Does It Work?
When you acquire new knowledge or undergo novel experiences, your brain cells (neurons) communicate through electrical and chemical signals. These interactions can strengthen existing connections or establish new ones.
Imagine this process as the growth of a tree's branches, expanding and becoming more intricate over time. For example, if you practice playing the piano, the neural pathways related to finger movements and music comprehension become more robust and efficient with continued practice.

C. Why Is Neuroplasticity Important?
Neuroplasticity is fundamental to our ability to learn and adapt to new situations. It is crucial for recovering from brain injuries, acquiring new skills, and refining existing ones. Without neuroplasticity, our brains would remain fixed and rigid, making it difficult to adapt to new experiences or recover from challenges.

D. Types of Neuroplasticity

- **Structural Plasticity:** This refers to the brain's ability to alter its physical structure in response to learning and experience. For example, research has shown that London taxi drivers have a larger hippocampus (a brain region involved in navigation) compared to non-taxi drivers.
- **Functional Plasticity:** This characteristic of neuroplasticity involves the brain compensating for

an injured area by reallocating functions to other brain regions. This is often observed in stroke patients who retrain their brains to perform tasks lost after the stroke. The application of neuroscience findings to support memory and learning illustrates the value of neuroplasticity in therapeutic contexts.

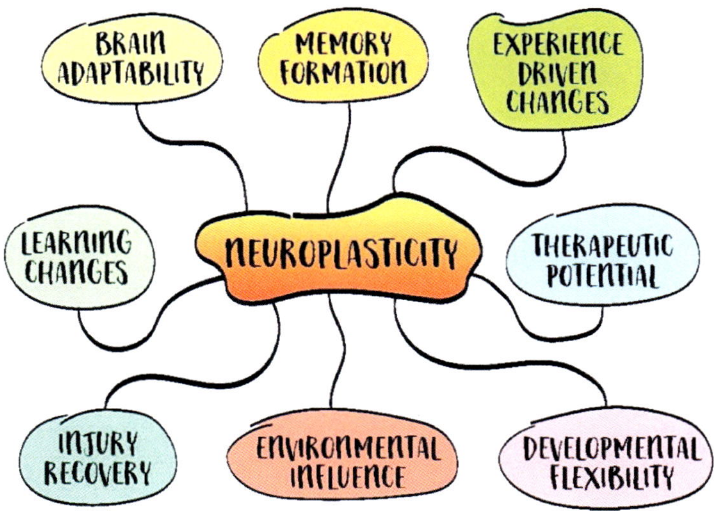

Brain Rewiring

Brain reorganization, commonly known as neuroplasticity, refers to the brain's remarkable ability to adapt, learn, and recover from injury. This dynamic process allows the brain to reorganize itself by forming new neural connections throughout life. Here are the key objectives of brain rewiring:

A. Enhancing Learning and Memory

- **Learning:** Neuroplasticity facilitates the creation of new neural connections in response to learning experiences. This adaptability ensures that individuals of all ages can acquire new skills and knowledge.

- **Memory Improvement:** By strengthening neural pathways through repeated use, neuroplasticity enhances the retrieval of stored information. This process is essential for forming both long-term and short-term memories.

B. Recovery from Brain Injuries
Following brain injuries such as strokes or traumatic brain injuries (TBIs), neuroplasticity allows the brain to compensate for damaged areas. The brain can reorganize itself and develop new neural pathways to help restore lost functions and abilities.

C. Rehabilitation
Neuroplasticity underpins many rehabilitation therapies. These therapies often involve targeted exercises and practices designed to help patients regain motor, cognitive, and sensory functions.

D. Adapting to New Experiences
Our brains are capable of forming new connections to adapt to novel experiences and environments. This flexibility enables us to manage changes and challenges, facilitating our ability to adjust to new circumstances.

E. Skill Development
Whether learning a new skill, mastering an instrument, or excelling in a sport, the brain's plasticity supports the development and refinement of complex skills.

F. Mental Health and Well-being

Cognitive-behavioral therapies leverage neuroplasticity to help individuals overcome negative thought patterns and behaviors. By repeatedly practicing new ways of thinking and behaving, the brain forms new, healthier neural pathways.

G. Emotional Resilience

Neuroplasticity contributes to emotional resilience by fostering positive experiences and coping strategies. Through this process, the brain can be rewired to better manage stress and emotional challenges.

H. Addressing Neurological and Psychiatric Disorders

- **Treatment of Disorders:** Therapeutic techniques such as EMDR for PTSD or various cognitive therapies for anxiety and depression utilize neuroplasticity principles to alleviate symptoms. These techniques help reshape the brain's response to stress and trauma.

- **Improving Cognitive Function:** In conditions like attention deficit hyperactivity disorder (ADHD), treatments aim to enhance focus and executive function. Neuroplasticity supports changes in neural efficiency and performance.

Brain rewiring is a fundamental process that supports continuous growth, adaptation, recovery, and enhancement in both cognitive and emotional well-being.

Leveraging Neuroplasticity for Learning

A. Continuous Learning and Practice

Neuroplasticity, the brain's remarkable ability to reorganize itself by forming new neural connections throughout life, is a continuous process, not limited by age. Engaging in novel and mentally stimulating activities is crucial for keeping your brain active and combating cognitive decline. What does this mean for you? To harness the power of neuroplasticity, keep your mind engaged by exploring new areas of knowledge and skill.

Consider taking up new challenges such as learning a foreign language, mastering a musical instrument, or engaging in a new sport. The key to benefiting from neuroplasticity is consistent practice. Every time you practice, you create and reinforce neural pathways, solidifying the new skill in your memory and enhancing your overall cognitive abilities.

B. Embrace Mistakes and Challenges

Mistakes should not be feared but embraced as a vital part of the learning process. Each error presents an opportunity for the brain to adjust and find more effective methods of performing tasks. Through trial and error, the brain refines its connections and improves its efficiency. Therefore, approach challenges with an open mind, view mistakes as learning opportunities, and use them to refine your skills and knowledge.

C. Stay Physically Active

Physical exercise is profoundly beneficial for both overall health and brain function. Engaging in activities that boost blood flow to the brain, such as walking, swimming, or practicing yoga, enhances neuroplasticity. Beyond its effects on brain health, exercise improves mood, reduces stress, promotes the growth of new neurons, and supports cognitive flexibility.

D. Get Plenty of Sleep

Sleep is a crucial time for neuroplasticity to thrive. During sleep, the brain reduces its information processing activities but focuses on organizing and strengthening neural connections. Adequate, restful sleep is essential for the brain to consolidate new knowledge and skills, enhancing learning and memory. Ensure you prioritize sleep to allow your brain to reorganize and solidify new information.

E. Mindfulness and Meditation

Practices such as mindfulness and meditation have been shown to positively influence brain plasticity. These practices reduce stress, improve concentration, and enhance the retention of new information. Mindfulness fosters greater awareness of thought patterns, enabling learners to adopt more positive and effective approaches to learning and personal growth.

F. Use Multiple Learning Methods

Incorporating various senses and learning methods can significantly enhance the learning process. For instance, when learning a new language, engage in reading, writing, speaking, and listening exercises. This multi-sensory approach stimulates different areas of the brain, leading to a more comprehensive understanding and retention of the material.

G. Stay Curious and Open-Minded

Maintaining a curious and open-minded attitude encourages the exploration of new ideas and perspectives. Engage in questioning, seek out new experiences, and remain receptive to learning from others. A curious mindset keeps the brain active and continuously adapting, which is vital for ongoing neuroplasticity.

H. Social Interaction

Active social engagement and maintaining strong social connections positively impact brain plasticity. Conversations and interactions expose the brain to diverse viewpoints and ideas, promoting cognitive flexibility and enhancing the capacity for new learning. Social exchanges keep the brain stimulated and adaptable.

I. Novel Experiences

Pursuing novel experiences and stepping outside of familiar routines are essential for stimulating neuroplasticity. New experiences, whether they involve visiting new places, taking up new hobbies, or learning new skills, challenge the brain to form and strengthen new neural pathways. Embracing the unfamiliar drives cognitive growth and adaptability.

J. Appropriate Nutrition

A balanced diet rich in antioxidants, healthy fats, vitamins, and minerals supports optimal brain function. Foods such as berries, fatty fish, nuts, and leafy greens not only bolster cognitive performance but also promote the growth of new neurons. Proper nutrition is fundamental for sustaining brain health and enhancing neuroplasticity.

K. Strengthening Your Connections

When you practice a new skill or study for an exam, your brain works diligently to fortify the synapses involved in that task. For instance, if you're learning to play the guitar, the synapses responsible for finger coordination and music comprehension become stronger. Continued practice enhances these connections, making it progressively easier to play the guitar.

L. Use It or Lose It

Conversely, if you cease using certain connections, they weaken over time. This explains why you might forget how to play a guitar song if you haven't practiced it for a while. The principle "use it or lose it" aptly describes this phenomenon. Your brain prunes away connections it no longer needs, ensuring efficiency and maintaining cognitive function.

M. Adapting to New Learning

Whenever you learn something new or encounter novel experiences, your brain undergoes changes. For example, if you start learning a new language, your brain begins to create new neural pathways and strengthen existing ones to comprehend new vocabulary and grammatical structures. This process, known as neuroplasticity, enables your brain to adapt and become proficient in the new language.

N. Adapting to New Information

Neurological plasticity extends beyond acquiring new skills; it also involves adapting to new information. For example, when you study for an exam, your brain actively forms and strengthens connections related to the subject matter. This process improves your ability to recall and apply the knowledge during the test, enhancing your overall performance.

O. Adapting to Damage

In cases of brain injury, neuroplasticity enables the brain to "compensate" for damaged areas by recruiting alternative regions to perform lost functions. For instance, after a stroke, patients often undergo rehabilitation to retrain their brains, aiming to restore abilities such as walking or speaking. This remarkable adaptability, where the brain adjusts to changes and damage, is attributed to neuroplasticity.

P. Enhancing Skills

The more you practice a particular skill, the more adept your brain becomes at executing that skill. Athletes and musicians, for instance, dedicate countless hours to practice because each session strengthens the neural pathways associated with their respective skills. Over time, this intensive practice refines their brains, allowing them to perform complex tasks with greater ease and precision.

In summary, neuroplasticity reveals the brain's extraordinary capacity for change and adaptation. By embracing strategies that stimulate neuroplasticity, you can enhance your learning abilities, improve skills, and better adapt to new challenges. Keep your brain active, explore new experiences, and enjoy the journey of continual growth and learning.

Breaking Free from Limiting Beliefs

The first step to overcoming mental obstacles is to acknowledge them. Recognize the most common cognitive barriers: self-doubt, fear of failure and perfectionism. These cognitive distortions can prevent you from developing and learning new practices. These negative belief systems are often deeply ingrained, limiting who you can become. Once you acknowledge these roadblocks, you'll be more likely to change your thoughts and behaviors, ultimately cultivating underlying resilience required for personal success.

Identify automatic negative thoughts and replace them with new, positive thoughts that support growth. Practice mindfulness exercises to see where your thoughts take you, ensuring judgment-free practice. See where your mind goes when it's left to wander. Train your mind to refocus on where you'd like your thoughts to go.

You can practice mindfulness by following these steps:

- Find a quiet space. If you can, find a seat where you are comfortable, close your eyes, and relax your body.
- Focus on your breath. Notice the sensation of your breath entering your body and leaving your body; if

any thoughts enter your mind, including thoughts about your breath, simply notice them and return to focusing on your breath.

- Notice your thoughts. Note any thoughts or feelings that arise without making any judgments about those thoughts or feelings; simply acknowledge them and return your attention to your breath.
- Be in the present. Continue to focus on the present moment; do not be concerned about yesterday or tomorrow.
- Practice mindfulness for at least 5 - 10 minutes every day to become more proficient at it.

Mental resilience is a result of breaking through mental barriers and redirecting thought processes. If you're able to understand your thoughts, intentions and what you allow to take up your very precious time, your life will become much more enjoyable than you could have ever planned for.

There are multiple practices for rewiring negative thoughts. Reframing negative thoughts and practicing visualization are just a few of those techniques. Each time you reframe a negative thought, you're perfectly retraining your brain for success and you're chipping away at the end of that mental barrier. Over time, this does not just break the mental barrier. It will start to empower you so that mental resilience ultimately becomes natural.

Rediscover the power of silence. Invalidating what's troubling you is incredibly empowering. Reframing negative thoughts consists of consciously changing your perspective about a situation. With reframing, instead of doubling down on self-defeating beliefs of "I can’t do this," you would rethink those into positive alternatives like, "This is difficult- but I am growing." This cognitive change increases your growth mindset and minimizes the emotional hardship of setbacks.

Visualization is the technique of mentally imagining what you want to happen. By creating a vision in your mind of what success looks like-whether it is giving a presentation or working on a new skill, you trigger your brain to go out and accomplish that. Visualization activates the same areas of the brain as if the experience were real, which builds confidence and motivation. Both reframing and visualization techniques act as a disruptor to negative thoughts and create a more resilient mindset.

Case Study on Overcoming Addiction and Mental Barriers

John had struggled with drug addiction since his late teens and had been in and out of rehab centers countless times, firmly believing that he was not able to break out of his destructive addiction cycle. His pessimism further reinforced these beliefs, causing him to relapse time and again. It was only during his last stint in rehab that he was introduced to mindfulness and the power of reframing negative thoughts.

Guided by his therapist, he learned how to spot when he was zigging himself. He practiced letting go of negative thoughts like "I'll never achieve this" and "I'll never resist a high". He also practiced visualizing himself as a person free from the need of drugs. With time, his mind strengthened, and it provided the tools to defend him against a relapse. This newfound mental clarity helped him resist cravings and face challenges with a calm, determined mind. With each small victory, John began to believe in his ability to overcome his addiction, eventually transforming his life and maintaining long-term sobriety.

CHAPTER 7

Neuroplasticity in Selected Cases

Neuroplasticity and ADHD: The Connection

A. Brain Structure and Function

Differences in Neural Connectivity: Research has shown that individuals with Attention Deficit Hyperactivity Disorder (ADHD) often exhibit distinct differences in brain connectivity and structure. Specifically, these individuals frequently have reduced connectivity between regions crucial for executive functions—such as attention, planning, and impulse control. For instance, the prefrontal cortex, a key area involved in these functions, may exhibit diminished connectivity in those with ADHD. This altered connectivity can disrupt the balance and efficiency of neural networks essential for cognitive control and regulation.

B. Brain Development

Delayed Maturation of the Prefrontal Cortex: Some studies suggest that the brains of people with ADHD mature more slowly, particularly in the prefrontal cortex, which is integral for executive functions. A delay in the maturation of this brain region can impede the organization of neural structures necessary for synaptic pruning and the development of effective neural networks. This delay can influence cognitive processes related to attention and behavioral management, potentially leading to difficulties in organizing and regulating thoughts and actions.

C. Role of Neurotransmitters

Dopamine and Neuroplasticity: Dopamine, a neurotransmitter essential for reward and motivation, plays a pivotal role in neuroplasticity. Individuals with ADHD often experience dopamine deficiencies, which can impact synaptic plasticity—the brain's ability to adapt and forge new connections. These deficiencies may hinder the development of neural pathways critical for maintaining attention and managing hyperactivity. Addressing dopamine imbalances can, therefore, be crucial for enhancing neuroplasticity and improving cognitive function.

D. Cognitive-Behavioral and Behavioral Interventions

Neuroplasticity-Promoting Therapies: Cognitive-behavioral therapy (CBT) and neurofeedback are interventions designed to foster neuroplasticity by establishing and reinforcing new neural pathways. Such therapies can significantly improve attention, impulse control, and executive functioning in individuals with ADHD. By targeting and modifying cognitive and behavioral patterns, these interventions can help in restructuring the brain's neural circuits to better manage ADHD symptoms.

E. Physical Exercise and Brain Plasticity

Impact of Physical Activity: Engaging in regular physical exercise has been shown to enhance neuroplasticity and cognitive abilities. Exercise stimulates the production of neurotrophic factors, which promote the growth and differentiation of new neurons and synapses. For individuals with traumatic brain injury (TBI) or cognitive impairments, routine physical activity can positively affect brain health and functionality, further supporting the development of new neural connections and improving overall cognitive performance.

F. Medication and Neuroplasticity

Stimulant Medications: Stimulant medications such as methylphenidate (Ritalin) and amphetamines (Adderall) are widely used in the treatment of ADHD. These medications work by increasing the availability of neurotransmitters, particularly dopamine and norepinephrine, in the brain. This increase can enhance attention, reduce hyperactivity and impulsivity, and, importantly, support neuroplasticity by fostering more efficient neural circuits. By optimizing neurotransmitter levels, these medications contribute to the brain's capacity for adaptive change and improved function.

G. Implications for Treatment

Understanding the interplay between neuroplasticity and ADHD offers valuable insights for treatment approaches. Interventions that promote neuroplasticity—including behavioral therapies, physical exercise, and appropriate medication—can help manage ADHD symptoms and enhance cognitive function. Ongoing research into neuroplasticity holds promise for developing innovative treatments that target the underlying neural mechanisms of ADHD more effectively.

By harnessing the brain's inherent ability to adapt and reorganize, we can create more effective strategies to help individuals with ADHD reach their full potential, improve functional outcomes and quality of life, and pursue independent, successful lives.

Helping Students with ADHD

Teachers and instructors can create a supportive learning environment for students with ADHD by employing targeted strategies and understanding their unique challenges. Effectively supporting college students with ADHD involves recognizing their specific needs and fostering an inclusive and accommodating educational atmosphere. Here are several strategies for educators:

A. Understanding ADHD and Training Awareness

- **Gain Basic Knowledge**: Familiarize yourself with ADHD, its symptoms, and its impact on learning and behavior. Attending workshops or training sessions focused on ADHD and inclusive teaching strategies can deepen your understanding and effectiveness.

B. Create a Structured Environment

- **Clear Instructions**: Provide clear and direct instructions for assignments, both in writing and verbally. This approach ensures that students fully understand the tasks at hand.

- **Consistent Routine**: Maintain a consistent routine in the classroom. Inform students in advance of any changes to the routine, allowing them time to mentally prepare.

C. Break Down Tasks

- **Chunking**: Divide large assignments into smaller, manageable tasks. Establish short-term goals and deadlines to help students remain focused and organized.

- **Step-by-Step Guidance**: Present tasks in small, manageable steps. Use lists or visual examples to further clarify instructions and support comprehension.

D. Flexible Teaching Methods

- **Varied Instructional Methods**: Incorporate a range of instructional methods, including lectures, group work, hands-on activities, and multimedia. Engage students through active learning strategies.

- **Allow Movement**: Permit students to move during long classes. Offer flexible seating options, such as standing desks or bouncy chairs, to accommodate different needs.

E. Provide Accommodations

- **Extended Time**: Offer additional time for tests and assignments. Provide a quiet, distraction-free environment for test-taking.

- **Note-Taking Assistance**: Provide options for note-taking support, such as outlines, guided notes, or access to lecture materials. Facilitate the use of technology-assisted memory aids.

F. Foster a Supportive Relationship

- **Encourage Open Communication**: Create an environment where students feel comfortable expressing their concerns. Schedule regular meetings to discuss their progress and any challenges they may face.

- **Positive Reinforcement**: Use positive reinforcement to acknowledge students' efforts and improvements. Provide constructive feedback that highlights both strengths and areas for growth.

G. Encourage Self-Management

- **Time Management Skills**: Teach and model effective time management skills, such as using a planner or other scheduling tools. Encourage students to track assignments and deadlines to develop organizational skills.

H. Promote Self-Advocacy

- **Encourage Self-Expression**: Support students in expressing their needs and seeking assistance. Help them connect with campus resources such as counseling centers, academic support services, and disability services.

I. Utilize Technology

- **Assistive Technology**: Introduce and support the use of assistive technology, including speech-to-text tools, organizational apps, and digital reminders. Employ educational technology that aids in engagement and organization.

Case Study on ADHD

Jake, a college freshman with promising prospects, had always harbored a keen interest in pursuing physical therapy. As he began his college journey, he quickly encountered significant academic challenges.

Diagnosed with ADHD in high school, Jake was aware that listening to lectures and managing his time effectively were his areas of struggle. Despite his sincere efforts, he found organization challenging, leading to missed deadlines and falling behind on assignments.

A. The Inception of Frustration

During Jake's first semester, his academic performance deteriorated sharply. The fast-paced college environment overwhelmed him. In lectures, he often found himself daydreaming, and when it was time to study, he struggled to concentrate. As assignments piled up, the fear of not performing to his best ability further obstructed his focus. This mounting frustration led Jake to question whether his dreams of a successful career in physical therapy were even attainable.

B. Identification and Help

Recognizing that he could not overcome these obstacles alone, Jake sought help. He reached out to Dr. Williams, his academic advisor, to discuss the difficulties he was facing. Dr. Williams devised a plan and coordinated with the campus disability services. Together, they created a tailored support plan that included extended test-taking time, access to lecture notes, and a quiet space for exams.

C. Learning and Application

Dr. Williams also recommended weekly meetings with a tutor specializing in ADHD. They crafted a structured study schedule with built-in breaks, varied methods to maintain engagement, and organizational tools to manage deadlines. Jake's professors were informed of his ADHD and adjusted their teaching methods to include clear, concise instructions and frequent summaries of their lectures. They also supported the use of assistive technology, such as note-taking apps and recording devices.

As a result of this comprehensive support, Jake began to make noticeable progress. The structured environment and personalized strategies helped him manage his time and concentrate better during lectures and study sessions. His grades improved, and he gained confidence in his academic abilities. By his senior year, Jake not only kept up with his coursework but excelled, receiving praise from professors and becoming a role model for his peers.

D. Achievement and Continued Success

Upon graduation, Jake crossed the stage with pride, diploma in hand. His journey didn’t end there; he set his sights on passing the national certification board exams for physical therapy. Applying the same strategies that led to his academic success, such as breaking down the test into manageable segments, taking regular breaks, and maintaining focus, Jake excelled in his certification exams.
Jake’s transformation from a struggling student to a successful college graduate and certified physical therapist stands as a testament to his determination and the efficacy of tailored support plans. His story offers hope to students with

ADHD, demonstrating that with the right guidance, understanding, and accommodations, they too can overcome challenges and achieve their dreams.

Neuroplasticity and Brain Injury

When someone experiences a brain injury, it offers a remarkable opportunity to observe the brain's extraordinary capacity for change and adaptation. Our brains, essential for thinking, learning, and remembering, can also modify and reorganize themselves in response to injury. This remarkable ability is due to the phenomena of synaptic plasticity and neuroplasticity.

In the context of recovery from brain injuries, it is crucial to understand how these processes facilitate healing and adaptation.

A. Synaptic Plasticity: The Rewiring of the Brain
Synaptic plasticity is fundamental to learning and memory, and it also plays a vital role in recovery following brain injuries. This process involves the strengthening and formation of new connections between neurons, which is essential for regaining lost functions.

B. Strengthening Connections
Following a brain injury, some neurons may be damaged or destroyed, disrupting neural pathways. Synaptic plasticity comes into play by forming new connections and reinforcing existing ones around the damaged area. For instance, if motor neurons are affected, the surviving neurons can forge stronger connections to compensate for the lost motor functions. This enhanced connectivity facilitates the recovery of motor skills.

C. Use It or Lose It

During rehabilitation, repetitive exercises act as stimuli to promote neuroplasticity. For example, in stroke rehabilitation, patients repeatedly attempt to move a paralyzed limb. This repetition helps to strengthen new neural connections, making the brain's pathways more robust and efficient for the intended movements.

D. Neuroplasticity, Reorganization and Adaptation

Neuroplasticity is crucial after a brain injury, as it allows the brain to compensate for lost functions and adapt to new challenges.

Neuroplasticity enables different parts of the brain to reorganize and assume functions of impaired regions. For example, if the left hemisphere, which is typically responsible for language, is damaged, the right hemisphere may take on some of these language functions. This adaptability helps patients regain cognitive abilities that were lost due to the injury.

E. Rehabilitation

Rehabilitation leverages neuroplasticity to aid recovery. Various forms of therapy, including physical, occupational, and speech therapy, utilize repetitive, task-specific exercises to stimulate neuroplasticity. For instance, after a traumatic brain injury (TBI), individuals might engage in activities that challenge their cognitive and motor skills, facilitating the formation of new neural pathways.

F. Cognitive Training and Stimulation

Cognitive stimulation exercises, such as puzzles, memory games, and problem-solving tasks, are beneficial for recovery. These activities engage brain areas responsible for cognitive functions and encourage neural growth and connectivity. For someone with a memory impairment due to brain injury, practicing tasks like recalling lists or solving complex puzzles can promote cognitive recovery.

Real-Life Examples of Recovery

Stroke Recovery

Neuroplasticity has been instrumental in the recovery of stroke patients. If a stroke damages the speech center of the brain, speech therapy can help other brain areas compensate for the impairment. With consistent therapy and practice, many stroke patients achieve significant recovery, regaining their ability to speak.

Traumatic Brain Injury (TBI)

Individuals with TBI can also benefit from neuroplasticity. Intensive rehabilitation programs help patients relearn fundamental functions such as walking, talking, and self-care. A notable example is Congresswoman Gabrielle Giffords, who sustained a severe brain injury from a gunshot wound. Through extensive therapy and rehabilitation, she made remarkable progress, illustrating the brain's ability to adapt and recover.

Neuroplasticity is relevant even in everyday situations and recovery from minor injuries. For instance, if someone temporarily loses their sense of smell after a head injury, the brain often reorganizes itself to restore this sense, demonstrating its remarkable adaptability.

Synaptic and neuroplasticity are crucial for recovery from brain injuries. By reinforcing and reorganizing existing connections, forming new ones, and adopting alternative roles, the brain can restore lost functions and improve over time. Rehabilitation therapies that harness these processes are essential for individuals seeking to return to their previous quality of life.

Case Study on Head Injury

John Smith, a daring 19-year-old college student, had a passion for adventure, with snowboarding being his favorite pastime. During a winter break with friends, John experienced a severe snowboarding accident. Despite wearing a helmet, he suffered a mild head injury, resulting in a concussion that affected his memory and cognitive functions. This period was particularly challenging for John, who had always considered himself academically gifted and dedicated to his studies.

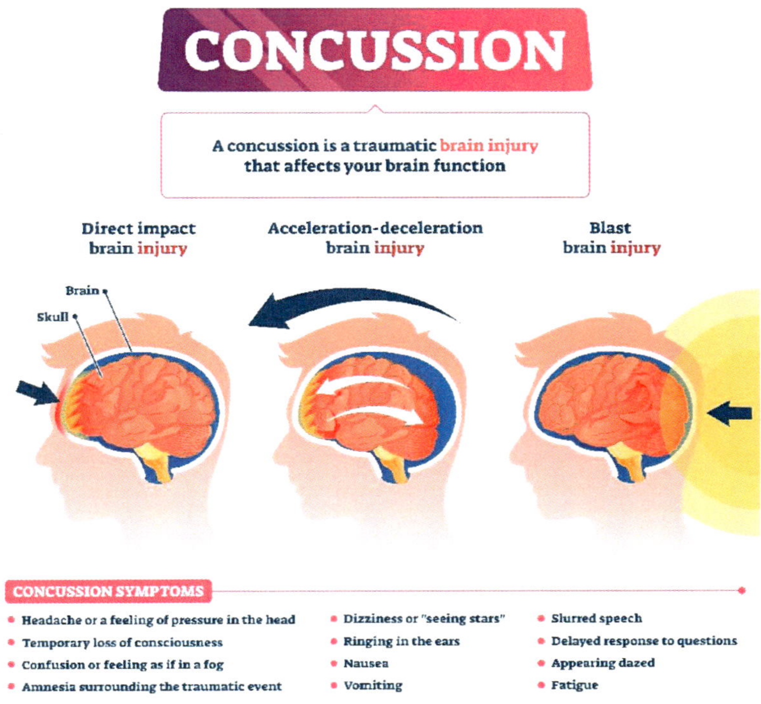

A. The Trouble

Following the accident, John faced significant difficulties with focus, information retention, and rapid thought processing. Tasks that previously took minutes now consumed hours. His frustration and anxiety about his academic future were palpable. Determined not to be defined by this setback, John embarked on a comprehensive treatment plan with specialists in head injuries. A key component of his recovery was cognitive rehabilitation, a tailored program designed to enhance memory, attention, and problem-solving skills. Additionally, John engaged in mindfulness and meditation practices to manage his anxiety and stress.

B. Academic and Peer Support

John's professors and academic advisors played a crucial role in his recovery. They provided additional resources, extended deadlines, and permitted him to record lectures for later review at his own pace. John also joined a study group, which facilitated social interaction and peer support. With the help of his family and friends, John implemented a solid plan to bolster his brain health. His new diet included omega-3 fatty acids, antioxidants, and vitamins known to support cognitive function. John also integrated routine physical exercise into his daily life, with light aerobic activities positively influencing his mood and cognitive processing.

Despite the considerable challenges, John's perseverance and effort led to notable progress. Over time, his cognitive abilities improved, allowing him to gradually return to his academic routine. He employed effective study techniques, such as breaking complex information into manageable chunks and using mnemonic devices and flashcards. John's dedication culminated in a remarkable final year of college, during which he not only caught up with his peers but also excelled academically. His achievements earned him recognition from his professors and several academic award nominations.

C. Graduation Day

On graduation day, John stood before his classmates as the valedictorian. He delivered a poignant speech on perseverance, the importance of seeking help, and the value of a supportive community. John's journey from a traumatic brain injury to a distinguished scholar served as an inspiring example for many. His story underscores the power of determination, effective strategies, and supportive networks in overcoming adversity.

John's experience is a testament to the incredible resilience of the human spirit and the brain's remarkable capacity to learn and recover. It also emphasizes the importance of never giving up, regardless of the obstacles faced.

Post-Traumatic Stress Disorder (PTSD)

Neuroplasticity is critical in understanding the development and potential treatment of post-traumatic stress disorder, a mental health condition that affects people who have experienced or observed a traumatic event or events. People with PTSD often experience flashbacks of traumatic events, anxiety, feelings of hypervigilance, and emotional numbing.

A. Traumatic Impact on Brain Structure

Trauma can change the way the brain forms and uses brain circuits, especially those in the amygdala (an emotional response center), hippocampus (a memory storage center), and prefrontal cortex (the control over decision making, thoughts and emotions). In PTSD, a person's neuroplasticity has been working on these areas, possibly making emotions seem more intense, leaving traumatic memories poorly imprinted, upregulating the emotional centers of the brain, and impairing memory and the ability to maintain control over emotional responses.

B. Maladaptive Differentiation of Circuits within PTSD

Going beyond simple flexibility, the concept of neuroplasticity underpinning maladaptive circuits suggest the capacity of maladaptive circuits to be "stuck" on, which implies an amygdala (which responds to fear) always on, and a prefrontal cortex that is off (which codes for an emotional modulation). Circuits acting in this manner have the capacity to support trauma or PTSD-type cognitive schema that reinforce negative thought patterns and desire for arousal-seeking behaviors.

C. Potential for Recovery Through Neuroplasticity

However, the brain can become less rigidly fixed through brain plasticity, and responses to trauma can be improved or changed through "relearning" or "rewiring". Psychological and physical treatments can capitalize on this plasticity and affect maladaptive circuits, proving a person can change in treatment.

PTSD treatments targeting different levels of neuroplasticity, or provide more balance in type of experience, activate responses, and resulting circuits during treatment, will likely be the most effective. Techniques known to engage neuroplasticity variants effectively to re-engage and better regulate under-engaged fear systems in the younger and threatened, trauma-focused cognitive behavioral therapy (CBT), eye movement desensitization and reprocessing (EMDR), and mindfulness-based therapies to reduce fear systems (hyper-activation), better regulate emotion expression, and resources.

D. Neurogenesis and Recovery

Newer research suggests that there is the possibility for neurogenesis (the creation of new neurons) from exercise, mindful meditation practice, medications, among others, in addition to traditional therapy, which could lead to restoration for those with PTSD. Engaging individuals in activities that allow for some possibility for the growth of new neurons could allow individuals to process traumatic experiences more efficiently, as well as develop healthier emotional responses. When considering the disruption of brain function likely to occur from experiencing trauma, neuroplasticity is still the leading discussion to represent the potential to change or repair. Therapeutic interventions can facilitate healing and enable individuals with PTSD to regain control of their emotional and cognitive health, by harnessing the brain's natural self-reorganization.

Cognitive Behavioral Therapy (CBT)

CBT is one of the most thoroughly studied and commonly used treatment strategies for PTSD. It focuses on the negative thoughts and behaviors that are related to and result from traumatic events. Patients in this type of treatment are forced to recognize the events and trauma from their lives, and work to through them in a structured pattern, which will lead to growth and evolution in treatment.

A. Challenging Negative Thoughts and Beliefs

The cause of and lasting effects of PTSD around the event are the negative thoughts that our feelings create. Chronic health issues from depression, anxiety and various other issues like chronic inflammation, pain, and immune system suppression will all be one issue after the next if we cannot begin to think and act on other thoughts.

B. Rewiring of Neuronal Circuits

Exposure therapies and challenging negative cognition are part of the process of what is called neuroplastic change or rewiring. In other words, behavioral practice enhances the function of the prefrontal cortex able to regulate arousal and fear response to the above event. At the same time, it weakens the connection with the individual amygdala, or anxiety-based conditional fears more strongly implicated in a PTSD activation.

C. Integrating New Learning
As the patient builds more broad or healthier pathways, the new learning built from pathway development supplants and increasingly utilizes the plastic pathways of cognition and behavior. In the process, to an extent, enhances neuroplasticity is as well. The process replaces old, non-healthy neural circuits for healthier ones that produce affective stability and cognitive flexibility.

Eye Movement Desensitization and Reprocessing (EMDR)

EMDR has also been getting a great deal of attention in the literature for the treatment of PTSD. Rather than somatic psychotherapy approaches which work the "bottom-up pathway" through the physical body, EMDR accesses the traumatic memory by recalling it and using bilateral stimulation of the brain with guided eye movement to help to process the memory in a less disturbing pattern. Some explanations on why this skill might result in a rewiring the brain include:

A. Memory Reconsolidation
Traumatic memories are laid down in a more fragmented, disorganized and emotionally charged memory state when they are "stuck". EMDR facilitates reprocessing traumatic memories and encodes into a more coherent and slightly less distressing memory.

B. Lowering Emotional Reactivity

EMDR seems to invoke less emotionality and cognitive and emotional pathology when reprocessing trauma. It fragments off the emotional memory or event from the cognitive memory and the entire human about themselves in some part of the brain. EMDR lays open and adjust the plasticity of the brain by assaying the emotional memory into new relational to create a response and build them out against which creates a new mental part for the reliving of the memories to flourish in this manner the memories become less aversive and bothersome in the long run.

C. Reinforcing Healthy Beliefs

EMDR does not just lead to desensitization of the memory in the way described above, but it also restores a positive, healthy image of the self or it corrects the special view of the self that is present in all PTSD.

Case Study on PTSD

The following case represents a detailed EMDR case illustration. Sarah, a 44-year-old police officer, had developed post-traumatic stress disorder (PTSD) after experiencing an armed robbery, where one of her colleagues was shot and killed. Sarah reported her life as 'falling apart' following these events. She was having daily nightmares, terrifying flashbacks, was too anxious to go near a bank or handle money in a shop, and she became obsessed with cleanliness and washing her hands.

Sarah's PTSD symptoms included:

- Flashbacks and nightmares about the robbery.
- Avoidance related to banks or any reminder of the robbery.
- Emotional numbness and detachment from her family.

- Constant hyperarousal with exaggerated startle response.
- Difficulty concentrating and sleeping.

Sarah was referred for a psychological assessment because she was unable to work and was not able to stand the sight of men. After reviewing the significance of trauma on Sarah's functioning, she was offered a course of EMDR.

EMDR Approach:

Sarah underwent several sessions of EMDR. As a result of these experiences, Sarah appeared to acquire the necessary adaptive information needed for the trauma and the associated intense emotions to be processed and diminished. With further bilateral stimulation, Sarah was processing the details and associations of the armed robbery. She now reported these scenes felt as if they were occurring in the past and felt "re-coded" into less traumatic memories. Sarah was able to walk to the bank and walked around the bank. Where she had started the EMDR process feeling panic-stricken, self-loathsome, and obsessed with cleanliness, Sarah was now feeling increasingly more connected to herself, with more self-worth, and a consistent level of pride.

CBT Approach:

EMDR initiated the desensitization of traumatic memories, but CBT also treated negative cognition and avoidance behaviors. Sarah held deep-seated beliefs that she was responsible for her friend's death and that it was her fault or even that there was something wrong with her. Suddenly, she had no sense of control, an illusion she was previously comfortably living with. These were unrelenting, pervasive, and anchoring on these faulty beliefs fueled her PTSD symptoms. CBT urged Sarah to begin dismantling these false beliefs. Sarah worked with her therapist to map out all the irrational beliefs and conclusions, which she came to hold post-trauma. This carefully crafted cognitive restructuring became the beginning on Sarah's journey to reformulate new neural connections. Sarah's amygdala became disconnected from her limbic system and initiated prefrontal cortex processing. The prefrontal cortex was the primary area in the brain contributing to enhanced cognitive control over her emotions and enabled her hippocampus to more adaptively process the context surrounding the accident with appropriate emotional tone.

Overall, by integrating CBT and EMDR, Sarah had a significant improvement in her PTSD symptoms.

Dementia and Alzheimer's Disease

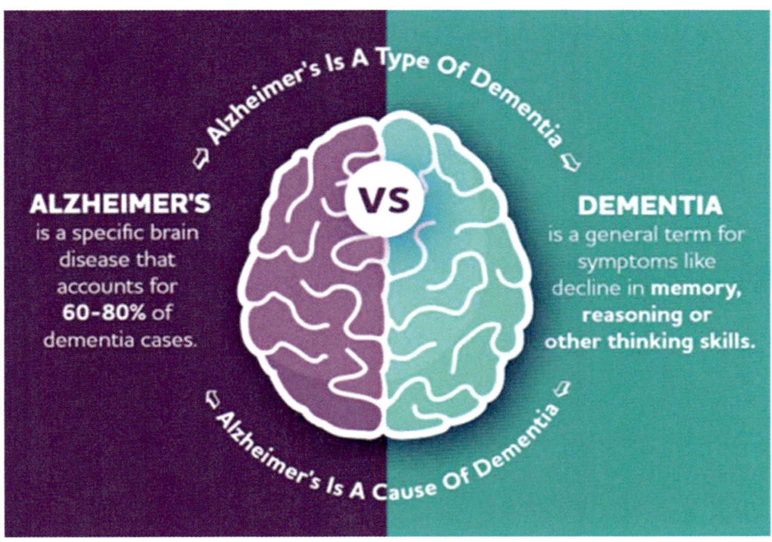

Dementia and Alzheimer's disease pose significant challenges, affecting memory, cognitive function, and daily living. Despite these challenges, the brain's ability to change and reorganize through synaptic plasticity and neuroplasticity offers hope. While complete recovery may not be feasible, improving quality of life and cognitive function is possible by leveraging these processes. Let's explore how synaptic plasticity and neuroplasticity can be harnessed to assist those with dementia or Alzheimer's.

Synaptic Plasticity and Neuroplasticity in Dementia and Alzheimer's Disease

A. Synaptic Plasticity: Strengthening Connections

Synaptic plasticity is the brain's ability to modify the strength and number of connections between neurons (synapses) based on their activity. In the context of dementia or Alzheimer's disease, synaptic plasticity involves the brain compensating for lost connections by reinforcing existing ones or forming new connections. Stimulating the brain through activities or therapeutic interventions can promote synaptic plasticity, helping to maintain cognitive functions despite the loss of connections.

B. Adapting and Reorganizing

For patients with Alzheimer's or dementia, this means that the brain can create new connections in different regions to take over functions lost due to the disease. Like synaptic plasticity, neuroplasticity can be stimulated through various interventions, leading to improved memory, thinking, and daily functioning.

Interventions and Strategies

A. Cognitive Stimulation Therapy (CST)

Cognitive Stimulation Therapy is a structured program designed for individuals with dementia. It involves engaging in activities that stimulate cognitive processes, such as puzzles, memory games, and group discussions. CST has been shown to enhance cognitive function and quality of life in those with mild to moderate dementia. The benefits are likely due to the stimulation promoting synaptic plasticity and neuroplasticity.

B. Physical Exercise

Physical exercise profoundly impacts brain health. It increases blood flow to the brain, stimulates the release of growth factors, and enhances neurogenesis. Activities such as walking, swimming, or yoga can foster neuroplasticity, potentially slowing cognitive decline.

C. Music and Art Therapy

Creative activities, including music and art therapy, can activate multiple brain regions and foster the creation of new neural connections. Engaging in activities such as playing musical instruments or painting can improve motor skills, memory, and emotional well-being, leveraging neuroplasticity to enhance overall cognitive function.

D. Cognitive Training

Cognitive training programs, often computer-based, offer targeted exercises aimed at improving specific cognitive skills like memory, attention, and problem-solving. These programs adapt to the user's skill level and provide appropriate challenges, promoting synaptic plasticity.

E. Social Engagement

Maintaining social connections and engaging in meaningful social interactions significantly impacts cognitive health. Social activities stimulate the brain and encourage neuroplasticity. Joining clubs, participating in group discussions, or volunteering can help maintain cognitive engagement.

F. Mindfulness and Meditation

Mindfulness and meditation practices have been shown to enhance brain plasticity. These practices can reduce stress, improve attention, and boost emotional regulation. Techniques such as deep breathing, guided meditation, and mindfulness exercises can be beneficial for individuals with dementia or Alzheimer's.

G. Supportive Environment

Creating a stimulating environment is crucial for promoting brain plasticity. This involves providing a safe, comfortable space filled with engaging items, such as puzzles, books, and familiar objects, to encourage cognitive activity.

H. Caregiving and Education

Educated caregivers who understand synaptic plasticity and neuroplasticity are better equipped to support their loved ones. They can create brain-healthy environments by implementing activities and strategies that address both the physical and emotional needs of the individual, promoting synaptic plasticity and neuroplasticity.

Neuroplasticity and Aging

Neuroplasticity, the brain's intrinsic ability to adapt by forming new neural connections throughout life, plays a crucial role in how we cope with aging. Several factors influence neuroplasticity as we age, including:

A. Reduced Neurogenesis

Aging is associated with a decline in the creation of new neurons, particularly within the hippocampus. This reduction can adversely affect memory and learning capabilities.

B. Neural Damage

Over time, the brain accumulates damage due to inflammation, oxidative stress, and other factors. This damage can impair neuroplasticity and contribute to cognitive decline.

C. Changes in Neurotransmitter Levels

Aging can alter the levels of neurotransmitters such as dopamine and serotonin. These changes can impact mood, cognitive functions, and neuroplasticity.

Promoting Neuroplasticity in Older Adults

To enhance neuroplasticity and maintain cognitive health in later years, consider the following strategies:

D. Be Active

Engage in regular physical activities, such as walking. Exercise improves blood flow to the brain, stimulates the release of neurotrophic factors (e.g., Brain-Derived Neurotrophic Factor, or BDNF), and supports the formation of new neural connections.

E. Cognitive Engagement

Participate in mentally stimulating activities like reading, solving puzzles, or acquiring new skills. Lifelong learning helps maintain neural networks and cognitive reserves, which can delay cognitive decline.

F. Interact with Others

Stay connected with friends and family and join community groups or clubs. Social engagement offers mental stimulation and emotional support, both crucial for brain health.

G. Eat Healthy

Follow a balanced diet rich in fruits, vegetables, whole grains, lean proteins, and healthy fats. Diets like the Mediterranean and DASH (Dietary Approaches to Stop Hypertension) are excellent choices.

H. Manage Stress and Sleep

Incorporate stress-relief practices such as mindfulness meditation and ensure you get quality sleep. Proper stress management and adequate sleep are vital for cognitive health.

CHAPTER 8

Future Frontiers of Learning

The future of learning is poised on the brink of a revolution, fueled by remarkable advances in neuroscience and educational technology. In this chapter, we will delve into these frontiers and their implications for education and training.

Advances in Neuroscience and Learning

A. Brain Imaging and Insights

Neuroscience is evolving rapidly, driven by advancements in technologies such as fMRI (functional magnetic resonance imaging) and EEG (electroencephalography), which allow scientists to observe the brain in real-time. These tools provide unprecedented insights into how various brain regions contribute to memory and learning. For instance, researchers can now track how different tasks activate distinct areas of the brain, shedding light on our information-processing mechanisms.

B. Personalized Learning

With a deeper understanding of brain function, personalized learning is becoming increasingly sophisticated. Imagine an educational platform that adapts to your individual learning pace and style. If you struggle with a particular concept, the system could offer additional resources or adjust its presentation to better suit your needs. Although this may sound like science fiction, AI-driven educational tools already exist that tailor lessons to the learner's progress and preferences.

C. Neurofeedback and Learning Enhancement

One of the most promising developments is neurofeedback, which involves providing learners with real-time feedback on their brain activity to enhance focus and cognitive performance. Neurofeedback functions much like a "fitness tracker" for the brain, using specific mental exercises to potentially improve cognitive functions, such as concentration, and thereby increase learning capacity.

D. Cognitive Training Games

There is a growing recognition that brain training games can be both enjoyable and beneficial. These games are designed to challenge memory, attention, and problem-solving skills, which can translate into improved task performance. Companies like Lumosity and Brain HQ offer games based on neuroscience research that aim to exercise and enhance cognitive abilities.

Research in Dementia and Alzheimer's Disease

A. Innovations in Cognitive Health

Ongoing research continues to uncover new opportunities for leveraging neuroplasticity and synaptic plasticity to combat cognitive decline. Future advancements may include technologies such as virtual reality and brain-computer interfaces, which could create environments enriched with diverse stimuli to promote brain plasticity in novel ways.

B. Potential for Cognitive Improvement

While dementia and Alzheimer's disease remain incurable, the application of neuroplasticity and synaptic plasticity offers hope for preventing or improving cognitive function and quality of life for those affected by cognitive impairments. Interventions such as cognitive stimulation, physical activity, creative arts, and social engagement can stimulate neuroplasticity and enhance personal satisfaction.

By focusing on environmental support and innovative technologies, there are numerous opportunities for personal growth and improved quality of life for individuals living with dementia and Alzheimer's disease.

Implications for Education and Training

A. Revolutionizing Classrooms

The classrooms of the future are set to transform dramatically compared to today's traditional settings. With the integration of advanced technology, students will have the opportunity to use virtual and augmented reality to delve into complex subjects in an immersive manner. Imagine exploring the bustling streets of ancient Rome through virtual reality or gaining insights into the human body by interacting with a 3D hologram of its intricate systems. Such innovative tools will not only make learning more engaging but also significantly enhance the interactivity of educational experiences.

B. Lifelong Learning and Career Development

In our rapidly evolving world, the concept of lifelong learning is increasingly critical. Continuous education has transitioned from being an option to a necessity for staying abreast of emerging industries and technological advancements. Online platforms such as Coursera, Udacity, and LinkedIn Learning offer diverse opportunities for individuals to acquire new skills and advance their careers at any stage of life. Neuroscience-based learning methods have validated that courses on these platforms are not only effective but also engaging, ensuring that learners remain motivated and informed.

C. Inclusive Education

Recent advancements in neuroscience are making it easier to provide inclusive learning opportunities for all students. By understanding the diverse ways in which individuals learn, educators can develop strategies that accommodate everyone, including those with disabilities. Tools such as text-to-speech software, customizable learning interfaces, and adaptive technologies ensure equitable access to quality education, promoting an inclusive learning environment where every student can thrive.

D. Data-Driven Education

The advent of Big Data and analytics has revolutionized how educators approach and enhance the learning process. Analyzing data on student performance, engagement, and behavior allows educators to gain a deeper understanding of effective teaching methods and areas needing improvement. This data-driven approach enables the personalization of educational strategies, thereby fostering individual student success and optimizing learning outcomes.

E. Advanced Teacher Education

Teachers will also reap the benefits of these educational advancements. Integrating neuroscience insights into teacher preparation programs can significantly improve the way educators design learning experiences. By incorporating findings from neurological research, teacher training can equip educators with the latest strategies for creating nurturing and productive learning environments, ultimately benefiting both teachers and their students.

F. Making Learning a Game

Transforming learning into a game makes the process not only enjoyable but also highly effective. Gamification involves applying game design elements, such as earning points and badges, to educational contexts. This creative approach fosters greater student engagement and motivates learners to overcome challenges. Schools and educational platforms are increasingly adopting gamified learning to keep students excited and invested in their educational journeys.

G. Real-World Applications

Education is increasingly extending beyond the confines of the classroom and into real-world settings. Programs that incorporate hands-on projects or internships alongside academic curricula provide students with practical experience directly related to their future careers. Neuroscience research indicates that applying learned concepts in real-life contexts enhances understanding and retention, making experiential learning a valuable component of modern education.

The future of learning is indeed exhilarating! With the continuous advancements in neuroscience and technology, the possibilities for education are boundless. By embracing these innovations, we can deliver more effective, inclusive, and engaging educational experiences. So, prepare for an era where learning is not just a necessity but an exciting adventure!

EPILOGUE

This is a testimonial letter from a former student sharing his story of recovery from a head injury. It serves as a powerful example of how the brain's incredible ability to adapt, known as neuroplasticity, plays a central role in learning, healing, and ultimately, success. He has given his permission to share his testimony in this book.

Finding My Way Back: My Success Story

By Chance Torres, RRT, RCP

After my head injury, I wasn't sure if I would ever regain my memory. It happened in late February of 2012 during a snowboarding accident where I hit my head and lost consciousness. I had fallen into a hole, making it difficult for people to find me. Eventually, I was rescued and rushed to the emergency room. After a series of tests, I was discharged with instructions to rest.

My instructor, Henry, had advised me to stay home for a few days, but the next day I decided to drive to school. While on the road, I became disoriented and couldn't remember how to get there. Panicked, I pulled over and called Henry, explaining my confusion. He reassured me, and I also called my girlfriend to pick me up. Together, we headed to school, but once I arrived, I realized I had forgotten even more—I couldn't remember where my classroom was or how to find Henry's office. I called him again, and he came out to meet me in the parking lot.

Henry walked me to his office, and as we talked, I realized I had forgotten that I was even enrolled in the Respiratory Therapy program. It was a frightening realization. But Henry, recognizing the situation, devised a plan to help me recover what I had lost. Over the following weeks, Henry spent countless hours tutoring me, reviewing the material, and guiding me step by step. I took my mid-term exams with several breaks in between to rest my mind, and I passed all my exams. His patience, dedication, and belief in my ability to recover were unwavering.

Thanks to Henry's relentless support, I slowly regained my knowledge and confidence. In December of 2013, I graduated from the program and earned my associate degree with high honors. I also received the Cory Sufrin Memorial Scholarship Award from the New Mexico Society for Respiratory Care. The award was based on scholastic achievements, character, and patient care ideals.

Without Henry's help, I wouldn't have been able to complete the program and become a registered respiratory therapist (RRT). My mother has been incredibly grateful for Henry's guidance, mentorship, and the unwavering support he provided during one of the most challenging times in my life. Today, I owe much of my career success to his incredible dedication and belief in his students—even when I had trouble believing in myself.

The Brain's Power to Learn, Adapt, and Heal

This is an example of neuroplasticity showing how the brain's ability can reorganize itself by forming new neural connections. Even after injury, the brain can recover and relearn lost information through consistent effort, practice, and support. In this case, the instructor's persistent guidance and belief in the student's ability to regain what he had forgotten were crucial to unlocking this potential. With every tutoring session and review, his brain was relearning and reinforcing the pathways it had once lost, slowly rebuilding the knowledge he needed to succeed in the Respiratory Therapy program.

The brain learns by repetition and reinforcement. When we review material, practice new skills, or even engage in mental exercises, we strengthen the neural pathways associated with those tasks. In this journey, the patience and structured approach provided acted as both the mental exercise and the encouragement his brain needed to adapt. With this help, his brain was able to re-establish the lost connections and build new ones to compensate for what was initially forgotten.

This experience not only taught him about neuroplasticity but also reinforced an important lesson for all learners: the brain is not static or fixed. It is dynamic and capable of change, even in the face of challenges like memory loss or injury. With the right support, persistence, and belief in its potential, the brain can overcome obstacles and thrive. His journey serves as a testament to this resilience.

Through neuroplasticity, we have the power to recover, relearn, and succeed—even when the odds seem stacked against us. The path forward is not always easy, but with dedication and the right guidance, we can unlock hidden potentials and achieve goals we once thought were out of reach. As you reflect on this story, remember that the brain's capacity for growth is within all of us. If someone could rebuild his future, so can you.

Student Engagement, Retention and Success

Student engagement and regular feedback are critical factors in promoting student retention and overall success. Engaged students are more likely to participate actively in their learning, develop a deeper understanding of the material, and remain committed to their educational journey. Active engagement can take many forms, from class discussions and group projects to hands-on learning experiences and interactive technologies, all of which keep students involved and invested in their learning process.

Hidden Disabilities

However, instructors must also be aware that some students may have hidden disabilities or personal challenges that make it difficult for them to participate openly. These students may be reluctant to engage fully in class discussions or activities due to anxiety, learning disabilities, or other unseen barriers. In such cases, encouragement and understanding from the instructor are essential. By creating an inclusive and supportive environment, instructors can help all students, including those with hidden disabilities, feel comfortable engaging and contributing at their own pace.

Regular feedback plays an equally crucial role in this dynamic. When students receive timely and constructive feedback, they are better equipped to identify their strengths and areas for improvement. This ongoing communication fosters a supportive learning environment where students can track their progress, set goals, and make adjustments as needed. Feedback not only helps students stay on course but also boosts their confidence and motivation, knowing they are making strides toward their academic goals.

Together, student engagement and encouragement for those with hidden disabilities, and regular feedback contribute to higher retention rates by creating a positive, responsive, and personalized learning experience. When students feel connected to their learning and supported in their efforts, they are more likely to persist, complete their studies, and achieve long-term academic and personal success.

APPENDIX A

Scoring and Interpretation

Learning Styles: Identify the dominant learning style based on the most selected options (a, b, or c).

Scoring:

- Mostly a) answers: Visual Learner
- Mostly b) answers: Auditory Learner
- Mostly c) answers: Kinesthetic Learner

Emotional Regulation: Assess how well you manage stress and emotional responses to learning challenges.

Scoring:

- Mostly a) answers: High anxiety/stress, needs stress management strategies
- Mostly b) answers: Moderate anxiety/stress, uses reflective strategies
- Mostly c) answers: Low anxiety/stress, resilient approach to setbacks

Attention and Focus: Determine your attention span and the effectiveness of focus-maintaining strategies.

Scoring:

- Mostly a) answers: short attention span, needs focus strategies
- Mostly b) answers: Moderate attention span, benefits from varied techniques

- Mostly c) answers: Long attention span, maintain focus with minimal strategies

<u>Cognitive Health</u>: Evaluate your sleep, exercise, and nutrition habits and their impact on cognitive performance.

Scoring:

- Mostly a) answers: low cognitive health habits, needs better sleep & exercise
- Mostly b) answers: Moderate cognitive health habits
- Mostly c) answers: Good cognitive health habits, maintains a healthy lifestyle

Recommendations Based on Results

Visual Learner:
- Use charts, diagrams, and written notes.
- Highlight key points and create visual summaries of the material.

Auditory Learner:
- Record lectures and listen to them.
- Participate in discussions and use mnemonic devices.

Kinesthetic Learner:
- Engage in hands-on activities.
- Use physical objects to illustrate concepts and take frequent, short breaks to move around.

Emotional Regulation:
- Practice mindfulness and relaxation techniques.
- Seek support when needed and maintain a healthy work-life balance.

Attention and Focus:
- Use structured study techniques like the Pomodoro Technique.
- Incorporate a variety of tasks to keep sessions dynamic and engaging.

Cognitive Health:
- Ensure adequate sleep, regular exercise, and a balanced diet rich in brain-boosting foods.
- Prioritize overall health to support cognitive functions.

APPENDIX B

Brain Learning and Adaptation Q&A

1. **What is neuroplasticity and why is it important for learning?**

Neuroplasticity refers to the brain's ability to reorganize itself by forming new neural connections throughout life. This capacity is essential for learning and adapting to new experiences. It allows the brain to compensate for injuries and diseases, and to adjust to new situations or environmental changes. Neuroplasticity underpins learning, memory, and skill acquisition, making it fundamental for cognitive development and recovery.

2. **How do neurons and synapses contribute to learning?**

Neurons, the brain's basic building blocks, transmit information through electrical and chemical signals. Synapses are the connections between neurons where this communication occurs. Learning induces changes in these synaptic connections, a process known as synaptic plasticity, which helps to strengthen or weaken them. This alteration enhances the brain's efficiency in retaining and recalling information.

3. **What role do neurotransmitters play in learning and memory?**

Neurotransmitters are chemical messengers that transmit signals between neurons across synapses. Key neurotransmitters involved in learning and memory include glutamate, which is essential for synaptic plasticity and long-term potentiation; dopamine, which is important for reward-based learning and motivation; and acetylcholine, which is crucial for attention and learning. These neurotransmitters facilitate the communication between neurons that underlies cognitive processes.

4. **How does sleep aid the brain's ability to learn and remember information?**

Sleep is vital for consolidating memories and processing the information acquired during the day. During sleep, particularly in the REM and deep sleep stages, the brain strengthens neural connections and transfers information from short-term to long-term memory. A lack of sleep can impair cognitive functions, reduce attention span, and hinder the ability to form new memories.

5. **What are some effective cognitive strategies for enhancing learning?**

Effective cognitive strategies to boost learning include:

- **Spaced Repetition:** Distributing study sessions over time to enhance long-term retention.
- **Active Recall:** Testing yourself on the material rather than passively reviewing notes.
- **Interleaving:** Mixing different topics or subjects during a study session to improve learning.
- **Elaboration:** Explaining and expanding on the material in your own words to deepen understanding.
- **Mnemonics:** Employing memory devices or techniques to aid in information retention.

6. **How can physical exercise benefit brain function and learning?**

Physical exercise enhances brain function and promotes neuroplasticity. It increases blood flow to the brain, releases neurotrophic factors such as Brain-Derived Neurotrophic Factor (BDNF), and encourages the growth of new neurons and synapses. Regular physical activity can improve cognitive functions, including memory, attention, and executive control.

7. How does stress impact learning and memory?

Chronic stress can negatively affect learning and memory by disrupting the function of the hippocampus, the brain region responsible for these processes. Elevated levels of cortisol, the stress hormone, can impair synaptic plasticity and the formation of new neurons. Managing stress through mindfulness, relaxation exercises, and regular physical activity can help mitigate these effects and support cognitive health.

8. How do emotional states contribute to learning?

Emotions play a crucial role in learning. Positive emotions, such as joy, curiosity, and motivation, can enhance attention, engagement, and memory retention. Conversely, negative emotions, including stress, anxiety, and depression, can impair cognitive functions like attention, memory, and decision-making. A review of neurological studies indicates that the amygdala, a brain structure involved in processing emotions, interacts with the hippocampus, the brain's memory center, during the learning process. Thus, emotions can influence memory by affecting the encoding and retrieval of information. Effective emotion regulation—through stress reduction, positive reinforcement, and fostering a supportive learning environment—promotes optimal learning outcomes.

9. What is the importance of synaptic plasticity in the learning process?

Synaptic plasticity refers to the ability of synapses to strengthen or weaken over time in response to activity levels. This process is essential for learning and memory formation. Long-term potentiation (LTP) and long-term depression (LTD) are key forms of synaptic plasticity that either strengthen or weaken synaptic connections, respectively. These adaptations enable the brain to efficiently store and process new information.

10. Can neuroplasticity support recovery from brain injuries?

Yes, neuroplasticity can facilitate recovery from brain injuries. After a brain injury, the brain can reorganize and develop new neural pathways to compensate for damaged areas. Rehabilitation activities that involve repetitive, task-specific training can enhance neuroplasticity and improve the likelihood of functional recovery. This process of adaptation and reorganization is crucial for reestablishing learned skills and cognitive functions.

11. In what ways is age related to neuroplasticity and learning?

Although neuroplasticity tends to decline with age, it remains active throughout life. Older adults may experience a reduced rate of neuron and synaptic proliferation, but regular intellectual and physical stimulation can help sustain neuroplasticity. Intellectual engagement, social interactions, and a healthy lifestyle throughout life can promote cognitive well-being and counteract age-related declines in brain function.

12. How does diet influence brain function and learning abilities?

Diet significantly impacts brain function and cognitive abilities. Essential nutrients such as omega-3 fatty acids, antioxidants, and vitamins are crucial for maintaining mental health. Omega-3s, found in sources like fish, nuts, and seeds, are vital for the health of neuronal membranes and neuroplasticity. Fruits and vegetables, abundant in antioxidants, help shield the brain from oxidative stress. Additionally, vitamins like B12 and D support cognitive functions and mood regulation. Adopting a well-rounded diet can enhance learning, memory, and overall mental performance by providing the brain with necessary nutrients for optimal functioning.

13. What is a circadian rhythm, and how does it affect learning and memory?

Circadian rhythms are natural, cyclical changes occurring approximately every 24 hours, essentially acting as a "biological clock" that regulates the sleep-wake cycle. These rhythms are influenced by external cues, such as light, and play a crucial role in regulating sleep patterns, which directly impact learning and memory.

How circadian rhythms impact learning and memory:

- **Timing of Learning:**

Circadian rhythms help determine the most effective times of day for learning and cognitive activities. For most individuals, cognitive performance and alertness peak in the morning and early afternoon, making these times optimal for learning.

- **Strengthening Memory:**

Sleep is essential for memory consolidation, and circadian rhythms regulate the sleep process. During sleep, the brain processes and organizes information from the day, which enhances learning and helps form lasting memories.

14. How can early detection and lifestyle changes help in managing Alzheimer's disease?

Early detection of Alzheimer's disease is crucial for management and potentially slowing the progression of the condition. Consider the following strategies:

- **Medical Interventions:**

After a diagnosis, medical interventions are available that may help manage symptoms and decelerate the disease's progression.

- **Cognitive Stimulation:**

Engaging in cognitive exercises, such as solving puzzles, reading, and playing memory games, can stimulate brain function and support cognitive health.

- **Healthy Lifestyle Choices:**

Adopting a healthy lifestyle, including regular physical activity, a balanced diet rich in antioxidants, and adequate sleep, can benefit overall brain health and may slow cognitive decline.

- **Social Engagement:**

Maintaining social interactions and participating in community activities can enhance emotional well-being and support cognitive function.

15. What are some effective strategies to reduce the risk of age-related cognitive decline?

Reducing the risk of age-related cognitive decline involves a combination of lifestyle modifications and proactive health measures:

- **Physical Activity:**

Engaging in regular physical exercise, such as walking, swimming, cycling, or dancing, boosts blood flow to the brain and supports overall brain health.

- **Mental Engagement:**

Participating in mental activities, such as learning new skills, pursuing hobbies, and solving problems, can strengthen cognitive resilience and delay cognitive decline.

- **Diet:**

Consuming a diet rich in fruits, vegetables, whole grains, lean proteins, and healthy fats provides essential nutrients for brain health. Foods high in omega-3 fatty acids, antioxidants, and vitamins are particularly beneficial.

- **Social Engagement:**

Staying socially active and maintaining relationships with friends, family, and community members can mitigate cognitive decline by providing emotional support and mental stimulation.

- **Stress Management:**

Employing stress management techniques, such as mindfulness, meditation, or yoga, can help alleviate stress and protect cognitive function from its long-term effects.

APPENDIX C

A Research Study

"Exploring the Link Between Synaptic Plasticity and Collaborative Learning for Enhanced Cognition"

COGNITIONIS Scientific Journal, Brazil on April 5, 2024

(first 3 pages, printed with permission from *Cognitionis*)

v.7 n.1 (202x) p. 181-196

Digital Object Identifier (DOI): 10.38087/2595.8801.354

EXPLORING THE LINK BETWEEN SYNAPTIC PLASTICITY AND COLLABORATIVE LEARNING FOR ENHANCED COGNITION

Henry Oh[1]
Fabiano de Abreu Agrela Rodrigues[2]
Eugene Demekhin[3]
Gabriel Lopes[4]
Howard Vince Oh[5]

ABSTRACT
This study attempts to investigate the important relationship that exists between synaptic plasticity and collaborative learning, and how this profoundly affects educational practices. Through studying the effects of flexibility on brain function and looking at teaching methods that involve collaboration, we are establishing the groundwork for improved, neurologically based educational strategies. Synaptic plasticity is a highly significant phenomenon in neuroscience, psychology education and clinical research.

Keywords: Synaptic plasticity. Synaptogenesis. Collaborative learning. Cognitive flexibility.

RESUMO
Este estudo busca investigar a importante relação existente entre plasticidade sináptica e aprendizagem colaborativa, e como isso afeta profundamente as práticas educative. Através do estudo dos efeitos da flexibilidade na função cerebral e olhando para métodos de ensino que envolvem colaboração, estamos estabelecendo as bases para estratégias educacionais melhoradas e baseadas neurologicamente. A plasticidade sináptica é um fenômeno altamente significativo na neurociência, no ensino da psicologia e na pesquisa clínica.

Palavras-chave: Plasticidade sináptica. Sinaptogênese. Aprendizagem colaborativa. Flexibilidade cognitive.

[1] PhD in Health Care, Associate Dean of Health Professions, Laramie County Community College, USA, Logos University International (UNILOGOS), Miami, Estados Unidos.
E-mail: director.henry@unilogosedu.org
[2] PhD in Neuroscience, Logos University International (UNILOGOS), Miami, Estados Unidos.
E-mail: drfabianodeabreu@gmail.com, Orcid: https://orcid.org/0000-0002-5487-5852
[3] EdD in Curriculum & Management, Logos University International (UNILOGOS), Miami, Estados Unidos. E-mail: professor.eugene@unilogosedu.org
[4] PhD in Education, Psy.D, Postdoctoral in Law, European International University, Logos University International (UNILOGOS), Miami, Estados Unidos.
E-mail: president@unilogos.edu.eu, Orcid: https://orcid.org/0000-0002-4977-5873
[5] MD, Associate Professor of Health Sciences, MD, Associate Professor of Helth Sciences,
E-mail: professor.howard@unilogosedu.org

1 INTRODUCTION

The human mind stands out as among the most engaging regions of scientific inquiry. It contains an intricate web of neurons and synapses that make it a very interesting network to study. Our ability to learn, adapt, and retain information is determined by synaptic plasticity which forms the core of this mystery. In essence, our cognitive processes are rooted in the dynamic and adaptive qualities of synaptic connections in the human brain. Thus, this biological setting helps us gather more knowledge or skill and recall such knowledge thus shedding light on how we grow and learn with our brains.

Going further into this subject matter takes us to how we can determine these changes in synaptic connectivity as they occur continuously. This is accomplished through extensive scrutiny of long-term potentiation (LTP), long-term depression (LTD) as well as other markers of synapse strength and changeability. This quest also brings us into the domain of augmentation where neuroscience meets education. This is where collaborative learning comes into play. The influence of peer interaction, cooperation, and collaborative problem solving on reshaping synaptic plasticity for cognitive outcomes are interrogated closely here.

1.1 PURPOSE OF THE STUDY

The main purpose of this study is to thoroughly analyze current research on the connection between synaptic plasticity, collaborative learning, and cognitive improvement. This entails consolidating findings from various studies in neuroscience, education, psychology, and related fields to uncover the mechanisms that underlie these phenomena. Through a critical evaluation of the literature, the review intends to inform educational practices, neuroscientific research, and interventions that strive to enhance learning outcomes and cognitive functioning in different populations and contexts.

1.2 SIGNIFICANCE OF THE STUDY

Synaptic plasticity is a key process underpinning learning and cognitive development in the brain. This process includes synapses, connections between neurons, and the ability to change and adapt in response to experience and stimuli (Meriney & Fanselow, 2019).

By studying synaptic plasticity, researchers can gain insight into the mechanisms underlying learning and cognitive processes. These insights can inform instructional practices and instructional strategies, as understanding how the brain learns and remembers can help educators develop more effective teaching strategies (Ramirez & Arbuckle, 2016).

Furthermore, synaptic plasticity studies can reveal the causes of neurodegeneration and potential therapeutic targets. Overall, understanding synaptic plasticity has important implications for learning and cognitive development. It can enhance teaching practices and instructional strategies, provide insights into the underlying mechanisms of learning and memory, and contribute to the understanding and treatment of neuroscience and psychology (Mateos-Aparicio & Rodríguez-Moreno, 2019).

2 LITERATURE REVIEW

2.1 SYNAPTIC PLASTICITY

The human mind and memory work by synapses. It is the ability of the connections between neurons to be reinforced or weakened because of activity. This is how neural circuits can make overall changes in their connectivity such that they are able to encode information and shape brain function. There are two main types of synaptic plasticity (LTP) – long term potentiation and (LTD) long-term depression. Long-term potentiation leads to the strengthening of synaptic connections after repetitive stimulation thus increasing signaling between neurons while on the other hand, LTD results from weakening synaptic connections often associated with low-frequency stimulation or prolonged inactivity (Bliss & Cooke, 2011).

Few aspects of cognitive function are not influenced by synaptic plasticity among which learning, memory formation, adaptation to environmental stimuli. Understanding synaptic plasticity gives insights into the neural mechanisms of learning and memory, as well as the neurodevelopmental processes of neurological disorders and cognitive dysfunction.

In general, synaptic plasticity is a dynamic and adaptive process that is basic to brain function and cognition. Synaptic plasticity's importance for cognitive processes cannot be exaggerated as it is a fundamental mechanism underlying learning, memory, and adaptation in the brain. Here are several key points highlighting its significance:

REFERENCES

Alban, D. (2024, February 19). 72 amazing human brain facts. Edited and medically reviewed by P. Alban, DC.

Barkley, R. A. (1997). Behavioral inhibition, sustained attention, and executive functions: Constructing a unifying theory of ADHD. Psychological Bulletin, 121(1), 65-94.

Barkley, R. A. (2006). Attention-Deficit Hyperactivity Disorder: A Handbook for Diagnosis and Treatment. Guilford Press.

Bear, M. F., Connors, B. W., & Paradiso, M. A. (2015). Neuroscience: Exploring the Brain (4th ed.). Wolters Kluwer.

Beck, J. S. (2020). Cognitive behavior therapy: Basics and beyond (3rd ed.). The Guilford Press.

Bjork, R. A., Dunlosky, J., & Kornell, N. (2013). Self-regulated learning: Beliefs, techniques, and illusions. Annual Review of Psychology, 64, 417-444.

Brown, P. C., Roediger, H. L., & McDaniel, M. A. (2014). Make it stick: The science of successful learning. Harvard University Press.

DuPaul, G. J., Weyandt, L. L., & Janusis, G. M. (2011). ADHD in the classroom: Effective intervention strategies. Theory Into Practice, 50(1), 35-42.

Erickson, K. I., Voss, M. W., Prakash, R. S., Basak, C., Szabo, A., Chaddock, L., & Kramer, A. F. (2011). Exercise training increases size of hippocampus and improves memory. Proceedings of the National Academy of Sciences, 108(7), 3017-3022.

Gazzaniga, M. S., Ivry, R. B., & Mangun, G. R. (2018). Cognitive Neuroscience: The Biology of the Mind (5th ed.). W.W. Norton & Company.

Hebb, D. O. (1949). The Organization of Behavior: A Neuropsychological Theory. John Wiley & Sons.

Kandel, E. R., Schwartz, J. H., & Jessell, T. M. (2013). Principles of neural science (5th ed.). McGraw-Hill Education.

Mackworth, N. H. (1948). The breakdown of vigilance during prolonged visual search. Quarterly Journal of Experimental Psychology, 1(1), 6-21.

Medina, J. (2014). Brain rules: 12 principles for surviving and thriving at work, home, and school (2nd ed.). Pear Press.

Mischel, W., Shoda, Y., & Rodriguez, M. L. (1989). Delay of gratification in children. Science, 244(4907), 933-938.

Oh, H., Rodrigues, F. de A. A., Demekhin, E., Lopes, G., & Oh, H. V. (2024). Exploring the link between synaptic plasticity and collaborative learning for enhanced cognition. Cognitionis Scientific Journal, 7(1). https://doi.org/10.38087/2595.8801.354

Prince, M., Bryce, R., Albanese, E., Wimo, A., Ribeiro, W., & Ferri, C. P. (2013). The global prevalence of dementia: A systematic review and meta-analysis. Alzheimer's & Dementia, 9(1), 63-75.

Scarmeas, N., Luchsinger, J. A., Stern, Y., Gu, Y., He, J., DeCarli, C., ... & Mayeux, R. (2009). Mediterranean diet and magnetic resonance imaging-assessed cerebrovascular disease. Annals of Neurology, 65(2), 211-221.

Shapiro, F. (2017). Eye movement desensitization and reprocessing (EMDR) therapy: Basic principles, protocols, and procedures (3rd ed.). The Guilford Press.

Sousa, D. A. (2011). How the brain learns (4th ed.). Corwin Press.

Sperling, R. A., Aisen, P. S., Beckett, L. A., Bennett, D. A., Craft, S., Fagan, A. M., & Phelps, C. H. (2011). Toward defining the preclinical stages of Alzheimer's disease: Recommendations from the National Institute on Aging-Alzheimer's Association workgroups on diagnostic guidelines for Alzheimer's disease. Alzheimer's & Dementia, 7(3), 280-292.

Squire, L. R., & Kandel, E. R. (2009). Memory: From Mind to Molecules (2nd ed.). Roberts & Company Publishers.

Van der Kolk, B. A. (2014). The body keeps the score: Brain, mind, and body in the healing of trauma. Viking Press.

Wilson, K., & Korn, J. H. (2007). Attention during lectures: Beyond ten minutes. Teaching of Psychology, 34(2), 85-89.

Zentall, S. S. (2006). ADHD and Education: Foundations, Characteristics, Methods, and Collaboration. Pearson.

Zhao, X., Yan, C., Zhao, L., & Shi, S. (2017). Neuroplasticity and behavioral mechanisms underlying the cognitive benefit of exercise in healthy older adults. Aging and Disease, 8(4), 486-504.

Zull, J. E. (2002). The Art of Changing the Brain: Enriching Teaching by Exploring the Biology of Learning. Stylus Publishing.

Made in the USA
Coppell, TX
12 July 2025